An Anthology
Of Recovery

Bernard Zeitler

An Anthology Of Recovery

ISBN: 10: 1533292825
ISBN-13: 978-1533292827

DEDICATION

This book is dedicated to all those who either want to understand an addict, are an addict wanting recovery or those who want to help. After writing several books on the topic and for the purpose of helping, it became clear that a one stop book could be helpful. This brought to fruition this Anthology which includes:

How To Win As A High Roller While Losing Your Shirt

The 30 Day 'Detox' For Gamblers

After Detox: The Next 90 Days

And

The Life Recovery Journal

Each is for a stage in recovery and each is a reference that can be looked back upon during times of difficulty.

An Anthology Of Recovery

CONTENTS

An Anthology Of Recovery

ACKNOWLEDGMENTS

This Book is a one stop resource for those who want to help others with recovery from addiction, those trying to understand and addict in their life and the addict who is working on recovery.

Each book can stand alone. While there is a table of contents it only determines where each book begins. While there may be some differences from their original layout, the intent of each remains.

Here is a description of each book:

How To Win As A High Roller While Losing Your Shirt

This book is intended to help understand addiction for both the addict and their loved ones. It addresses why a person can't 'just stop' and the back story of addiction from several different potential directions.

The 30 Day 'Detox' For Gamblers

This book, while listed for gamblers can be used for any addiction or the person who is affected by the addiction. It helps focus on the aspects of recovery that are set in the mind. Addiction has a reward system and for recovery we need to set up a change in how we think about those rewards. This book works on a principle of focusing on a thought each day and writing about it.

After Detox: The next 90 Days

This book expands on that 'Detox' process and gives help in getting the change to stick through the process of further training.

The Life Recovery Journal

This is a Journal for continuing the work of recovery after 'Detox' has been expanded and the habit needs to be given support. It is also the largest of the 4 books in the anthology.

While each book is available individually, this book is here to allow for less expensive access to the resources so that it can be followed through with consistently.

Bernard Zeitler

HOW TO WIN AS A HIGH ROLLER WHILE LOSING YOUR SHIRT

INTRODUCTION

What is your dream? What would you do if your dream came true? Compulsive gamblers go beyond all that. I know because I am a recovering compulsive gambler. My goal in writing this book goes beyond the story to the fantasy and how it looks over time, both in recovery and as the addict goes down the proverbial rabbit hole.

My name is Bernie, and I am a compulsive gambler. My chosen form of gambling – scratch off tickets. My last 'bet' was on November 21, 2007, yet I look back over my life and recognize early signs going back to about third grade.

To explain my recognition of childhood gambling signs, I first need to give the definition of Compulsive Gambling. Gambling is, as defined by GA (Gamblers Anonymous):

Any betting or wagering, for self or others, whether for money or not, no matter how slight or insignificant, where the outcome is uncertain or depends upon chance or "skill."

That being said, during my childhood, I played marbles, go fish, and other games. I also took on other challenges such as eating, drinking (pop), and anything else for gain or personal recognition. These of themselves do not indicate compulsive gambling.

However, when taken too seriously, they can indicate a problem in the making. The combination of the challenge and the thrill of competition helped promote the compulsion. When I was young, I played the games without any competitive focus until the challenge started to be a way to be accepted. When I was the winner, I received recognition. It became so enjoyable to be recognized for an accomplishment. It is difficult to believe that eating more food or drinking more soda pop than friends or class mates would give anyone a 'high,' but that is what began to happen.

Here is where I begin with the childhood high of being recognized for being better at something. In school, most of us just blend in. Even an athlete can find themselves blending into a bigger pool of all the area school athletes. One might stand out in a class of 25, but is that as far as it goes? Most people want to be appreciated at some level, but at what level does it stop? Sometimes even appreciation doesn't stop the desire to be the best. Compulsive gamblers and addicts go beyond that level to an escape from the life they are living. I will look at the process by following a poem I adapted from the poem: "Autobiography in Five Short Chapters" by Portia Nelson and with my original articles.

After that, I will expand and talk about the newest lessons learned.

This is my adaptation for addiction and recovery....Insert chapter one text here.

ADDICTION AND RECOVERY IN 5 SHORT CHAPTERS

1.

I head toward my
addiction. The
addiction is a deep
hole
I fall into it.
I am lost... I feel helpless.
I blame others.
It takes forever to escape it.

2.

I head toward the addiction again.
The addiction is still a deep hole.
I pretend it does not exist.
I fall into it again.
I can't believe I am back in the hole, but I still
blame others. It again takes forever
to escape.

3.

I head toward the addiction again.
I see the deep hole of addiction.
I pretend it is not there.

—

I still fall in ...it is a patterned habit.
I see it clearly.
I know this place.
I take responsibility for it.
I escape immediately.

4.

I head toward the addiction again. I see the deep hole of addiction I avoid it at the last second.

5.

I change my path avoiding the addiction entirely.

—

SUMMARIZING MY 5 CHAPTERS

1.

I head toward my
addiction. The
addiction is a deep
hole
I fall into it.
I am lost... I feel helpless.
I blame others.
It takes forever to escape it.

This is the early process of the addiction. At this point, I am beyond the wish to stand out or be special. There comes a point where getting the high is all that matters and compulsive gamblers are no different. They chase the win with no regard for what happens at the end of the process. It does not matter how many other times they have been there... It only matters that the results are the same, yet they expect them to be different. There is no acknowledgment of having a problem, and when the gambling has run its course, it is a hole that causes the gambler to look for a way out and find scape goats to take the blame.

I lose because I do not have the best plan. No one is there to bring me luck, and yes, I cannot go home because no one cares. I couldn't find my way, and I feel hopeless. It is not my fault everyone else is not supportive or does not understand. Since I am not at fault, it is harder to find my way out, and often, I begin planning my return to 'win' my way out of this mess.

2.

I head toward the addiction again.
The addiction is still a deep hole.
I pretend it does not exist.
I fall into it again.
I can't believe I am back
in the hole, but I still
blame others.
It again takes forever to escape.

There comes a time when addicts know that they are heading for trouble but don't want to believe it, so they keep going. Compulsive gamblers, like any addict, get to that point where chasing after the high is all that matters, even if they know that the letdown is coming. Here I am, gambling to escape the reality, and when I get to the letdown, I tell myself I did not see it coming. The reality is: I knew it was coming. I just ignored it, so when it happened, I could still blame others. At this point, addicts never really get out of the mess, but they do see an improvement to a plateau. At this point, others are beginning to see what is happening. However, the addict pretends that the problem does not exist, and those around the addict often don't know exactly what the problem is.

—

It is my experience that this is a place where the addict is stuck for a long time.

3.

I head toward the addiction again.
I see the deep hole of addiction.
I pretend it is not there.
I still fall in ...it is a patterned habit.
I see it clearly.
I know this place.
I take
responsibility
for it. I escape
immediately.

This is the point at which the addict knows what is coming but does not look at it. I know what is coming. I know that it is a disaster, but I focus on the high. I ignore the past history until I get into the disaster. Once there, I take responsibility and get out of my mess. The problem, though, is that as long as I can see the next high, I'll go back. I have figured out my pattern and live as if it is all worth it. This can go on for years, and as with other addictions, the addict can revert to earlier chapters.

4.

—

I head toward the
addiction again. I see
the deep hole of
addiction I avoid it at the
last second.

This is the beginning of recovery. The addict knows
s/he has a problem, and while s/he still heads down
the path of destruction, s/ he stops at the last second.
It does not mean they don't use, but they stop as soon
as they start. It does not get to the depth that it has in
the past. Oddly this is the most dangerous stage of all
because it is where 'slips' happen. Often, it is a point
at which the addict is most disappointed with
themselves. I had an experience with this after my
first GA meeting which left me with a desire to never
go back to that. Here is a great example of this
chapter... I went to my first meeting, heard all the
stories, passed the test but decided I was not that
bad. So as a result I left the meeting and went directly
to the convenience store to buy a scratch-off ticket. At
the moment I purchased that ticket, I not only knew I
had a problem but knew I did not want to go back
down that path.

5.

I change my path, avoiding the addiction
entirely.

This is the point where recovery is in place. The
hardest part of recovery is not getting too confident

—

in it. The paths addicts take changes, but even then, there are things to look out for. Even when they change the road they take, there can be potholes and road construction, so watching the new road requires the full attention of the addict just like driving on the road. It is likely that if the addict doesn't stay alert, they will either go back to the original addiction or pick up a new one. In the following pages, I hope to reveal my path in a way that shows what other addictions can move in to replace the old one.

Join my journey into the addiction world and what happens in recovery. Let's look at how you can win as a high roller while losing your shirt of denial. We will begin with the fantasy of the compulsive gambler.

The Fantasy World

The fantasy of the compulsive gambler in the beginning is that they will be able to win big and help make life easier for others and themselves. The dream is truly a fantasy that rarely becomes a reality. For me, there was no reality for the fantasy, and it went to the place no one looks at in life.

When someone starts to plan for the future, no one says "oh I'll bury myself in debt" or "It would be fun to be broke." I started gambling in high fashion when I started seeing a day when I would no longer have to worry about what my job was. I began to believe that I'll win enough big bets to take care of

—

everything. Over time, the fantasy became a false reality for me.

When I was in high school, the state was just starting their lottery programs, and I would buy one every so often but really focused on other stuff. My addiction at that time was just for fun and continued for almost two decades as such. During that time, I tried smoking, alcohol, and dealt with an eating problem. I still struggle with overeating, but I never let the other stuff get a hold of me enough. As time went on, I found myself enjoying the time scratching off the tickets. I never really had the patience for the lottery drawings.

It started at some point with a "few minutes" of scratch-off tickets before I went home. How realistic is it to believe that I was going to hit the big win? Looking back on it, I wish that lightning would have struck before November of 2007, but it did not happen that way. The fantasy of winning big is less likely than being hit by lightning, but most, if not all, gamblers begin with the fantasy of beating the odds. Once I started actively chasing the dream of a big win, I was off to the races. Looking back, I wish I had never entered the race. In November 2007, I had won that race. I started to recover from the biggest most self-destructive problem in my life. Today, I still fight for a recovery that is one day at a time and sometimes one minute at a time.

The "chase" is a fantasy world that deals with a selfish side of life. I felt guilt because of my own failures, and ultimately, this low self-image drew me deeper into the "chase." Gambling was my escape

—

from arguments and the feelings of inadequacy. I could play scratch offs and enter a dream world of being someone special. I could escape into the wood work for a short period. Twenty, thirty or forty dollars or more later, I'd head home knowing that my ex-wife would be asleep, and I felt I would get peace. To this day, I fail to understand how my gambling comforted me, yet I know it did until the very last bet.

My fantasy world came crashing down in late 2007, and now I am trying to build my life on realities as best I can. I looked to gambling to provide solutions for problems ranging from self-esteem to companionship. My ex-wife had told me that I had an affair with gambling and I cannot deny that. I deluded myself by dreaming of giving my family security financially through gambling in the beginning, yet at some point, the "chase" became my best friend, my lover, and a part of who I was.

The fantasy is over for me that I'll provide for my family all they need through my lover – the scratch-off ticket.

Thoughts and Reflections

Clean day Jan 25, 2018

Bernard Zeitler

Thoughts and Reflections

Thoughts and Reflections

MY WALK OF RECOVERY AND
THE PAIN THAT SURFACED

I am a compulsive gambler and have an addictive personality, which means that I must work on having a higher awareness of what I am doing and know my weaknesses. As a person with an addictive personality, I can easily fall back into an addiction even if it is not the one I am recovering from. People have said that addiction is hereditary, and this is only half true. It is not addiction that is hereditary, but the tendency to be addicted. Below is my story after which I will discuss where I am in recovery today. I have heard it said by others: "Addiction is Addiction is Addiction." No matter what the addiction, it is all the same. For that reason all addicts have to be aware of the triggers that could start them on the path to a new addiction.

I have to agree with the idea that once someone has been addicted to anything, they have to watch out for cross-addiction. For example, when a smoker quits smoking, they often begin to over eat. If an addictive personality begins the recovery process, they must become aware of the possible substitutions that may come into play. While addiction has a genetic component, it can and usually is triggered by an initial choice to try that which is the addiction of choice. Before an addiction can happen, there has to be an exposure situation which means that the person has to have an experience. Oddly enough, it does not have to be a good experience to result in the addictive behavior.

I can look back over the years and see that I've been addicted to a number of things. The recovery I am going through today is from gambling. Much of addiction starts off as a past time. It's all in fun. Most addicts, myself included, say it all started with a recreational action. For instance:

- I'm only a social drinker.
- I only spend a little on gambling.
- I just tried one joint.
- I am only doing this because of peer pressure.

- I only smoke once in a while.

The problem is that once an addiction starts, the addict builds up a tolerance, and it takes more to achieve the same feeling. People start to relax and get away from problems for a while. Ultimately, the excuses start. Two such excuses are:

I don't have a problem.

I am a responsible... (drinker, gambler ect.)

This covers up the problem because as I said, the tolerance levels go up.

My addiction to gambling started as just one ticket and grew into a problem over time. Early on I was a 'binge' gambler, but as time went on, the 'binges' became more frequent and more expensive. By the end, it was no longer just 'binging' it was an almost continuous desire for the gambling.

Gambling: The Pit at The End of The Road

In late 2007, I came home from work a lost soul. My gambling had been out of control for many months, and now I had been sent home from work to await my fate. I was looking at being fired because of cash drawer shortages. My manager at the time knew I did not steal and was a good worker. He told me who to contact in order to fight for my job back. Over the next two days, I did fight for my job and was kept with the company. However, it meant that I would be moved to a different store.

A few days after losing my job, I was reinstated and scheduled to return to work at a new store. After a few years more working there, I left the job. I ended up spiraling down into a deep depression and before returning to work in 2007, I was admitted to the Adult Psych Ward for Suicidal Depression. This would be my home for ten days, and I spent the time working on returning to "normalcy". By the time I was admitted, I had "come clean" with my ex-wife about gambling. I was mortified because during our short courtship and the early years of our marriage (from 1987 to1995), I watched my mother-in-law spend excessive amounts of money on scratch-off lottery tickets and swore I would never do that. The problem was that now I had become the very thing I swore I would not. On this day my ex-wife saw the pit of my depression that I had struggled with for years. She did not see the level of depression that was often there, but in November of 2007, it was all out in the open, and during the ten days I was out of the house, she grew to our the home as calmer. She discovered by cleaning out my car, looking at finances, and doing the math just how bad things were because of my addiction. I on the other hand was still in denial of the problem being *all* mine in this area. Gambling can start as a past-time and not be a real problem, but it can and often does change suddenly. I remember gambling a little since being in high school. Through to 1995, it was clearly not a problem because I may have spent all of $5.00 to $10.00 a year on this stuff with the rare increase to as much as $30.00 a year. The problem was that at some point, I became blind to my gambling and did it to escape my problems in the marriage. On November 16, 2007 (my mother's birthday), I was discharged from the adult Psych Ward and returned home a smaller person with less depression and on medications for Bipolar disorder because the cloud of depression had been lifted. I look back on that ten days as a turning point for me while I still have a long way to go, this time, I'd changed my path.

On November 21, 2007, I attended my first GA meeting and proceeded to spend $1.00 on a scratch off ticket after the meeting. This also was a turning point for me. My thoughts when I left that first meeting were that I do not really have a problem. When I purchased that $1.00 ticket, I crumbled because I saw the lie of "I don't have a problem." Since that day, I have not had the urges like I had been, and whenever I start thinking I have licked the problem, I remind myself of that first GA meeting and of the ten days in Adult Psych.

Bottom line if a person denies having a problem but has the symptoms, they are only hurting themselves in this denial. The gambling, however, hurts family, friends, and work. Beyond this, it hurts all of society ultimately because of the things that tend to happen as a result.

If someone you know or you gamble, ask these Twenty Questions in regards to them or yourself:

(These are the questions asked of all new members of Gamblers

Anonymous)

- Did you ever lose time from work or school due to gambling?
- Has gambling ever made your home life unhappy?
- Did gambling affect your reputation?
- Have you ever felt remorse after gambling?
- Did you ever gamble to get money with which to pay debts or otherwise solve financial difficulties?
- Did gambling cause a decrease in your ambition or efficiency?
- After losing, did you ever feel you must return as soon as possible and win back your losses?
- After a win, did you ever have a strong urge to return and win more?
- Did you often gamble until your last dollar was gone?

- Did you ever borrow to finance your gambling?
- Have you ever sold *anything* to finance gambling?
- Were you ever reluctant to use "gambling money" for normal expenditures?
- Did gambling make you careless of the welfare of yourself or your family?
- Did you ever gamble longer than you had planned?
- Have you ever gambled to escape worry or trouble?
- Have you ever committed or considered an illegal act to finance gambling?
- Did gambling cause you to have difficulty sleeping?
- Do arguments, disappointments, or frustrations create within you an urge to gamble?
- Did you ever have an urge to celebrate any good fortune by a few hours of gambling?
- Have you ever considered self-destruction or suicide as a result of your gambling?

Further have you ever thought any of the following?

- "The next one is a winner."
- "I know I'm getting close."
- "I can stop whenever I want."

- "I need to win today because I need the money."

I answered the twenty questions with some clarity but later realized and now remind myself daily that the truth is that all twenty questions are true when I am honest with myself. When I answered them the first time publicly, I answered **False** to about five. If you are a gambler or know someone who is, be honest with yourself because while gambling that is the biggest challenge. Gambling starts out as a choice but becomes a hunger until the problems pile up and the truth hits. The Twenty Questions are asked of every new member of Gamblers Anonymous. It is said that most gamblers will answer yes to at least seven of them (that is less than 50%). My experience is that in the long run, many of us could see our life through a yes to all Twenty Questions. The statements are things I've told myself to justify my actions.

What is really sad is that I lied to myself and believed the lies. Many gamblers are liars who lie to themselves so well that they begin to believe the lies. It is necessary to cover oneself when gambling mostly because deep down, they know that what you are doing is wrong. My biggest challenge since starting on the road to recovery has been being honest with myself and those closest to me. The biggest loss is my ex-wife's trust. I may never get it back, and even today, there are struggles to battle the anger I have at myself. The anger was projected often on to my ex-wife because I no longer had any control of finances. I battle to regain my own self-respect and individualism while I was feeling trapped and hopeless about my marriage relationship. Recovery for a gambler is like trying to cut off a diseased appendage in the Old West.

Bernard Zeitler

Thoughts and Reflections

Thoughts and Reflections

ADDICTION: THE SUM TOTAL OF RECOVERY

My addiction to gambling started as just one ticket and grew into a problem over time. Early on I was a 'binge' gambler but as time went on the 'binges' became more frequent and more expensive. By the end it was no longer just 'binging' it was an almost continuous desire for the gambling. I note a number of points that are now going to be revisited. I noted the government's part in the addiction to gambling. This applies to any legal addiction. The list below is of legal and accepted addictions.

- Alcohol
- Smoking
- Gambling

This is not a complete list, but these three alone bring in more tax revenue for government entities equal to or greater than any taxes on income.

In Michigan, alcohol sales are connected to liquor licenses, sales taxes, and hidden taxes related to sales buried in the price of the alcohol, and let's not forget DUI and other tickets that can be issued as a result of the consumption of alcohol. Likewise many Alcoholics smoke as well as the two addictions go together. Remember how you used to go to a bar and people would also be smoking.

Cigarettes are sold at prices that are close to 60% taxes and then on top of that, there is a state sales tax. Since Gambling has become legal it has proliferated in the bars so it would seem that all three were together for al long time. As smoking was cut back in public places Gambling seems to be growing in the form of Club

Keno, Card Games and people who are watching games they have wagers on.

The lottery is a significant income maker because the majority of the money brought in is profit. Retailers are not making much on this revenue item unless the winning tickets are sold there.

Casinos are another avenue for profit as the Government has to approve those not operated by Indian Tribes and even those run by the Indians have payouts for the government. These are things I see in recovery which have supported the idea that some addictions are acceptable to government agencies because they make money on the addict's misfortune. The more I use or do the behavior the more the money comes in to government coffers.

It is sad that often addicted individuals don't realize the problem until they are at the lowest possible point. I vowed not to be like my mother-in-law and yet today I am recovering from the very addiction she had. All addiction ultimately leads to the same places — Prison, Insanity, or Death. My path to recovery travels through insanity.. Gambling made my depression worse ultimately. It drove me to a place of insanity. I created my own prison that I am still working to be released from today. Not all prisons are buildings. For example, I am in the prison of failure because of gambling. What I mean by a prison of failure is that personal character flaws and past mistakes have been a stumbling block in my marriage, my relationships with family members, and my job situations. The gambling that I did overshadows my daily life. My ex-wife no longer trusts me, and my sons, who already did not like me, have a greater aversion to me, and I almost lost my job over gambling.

The cost of gambling is so great that it brings down even the best of people. The jobs it creates are more than just the obvious ones at the casinos and lottery commissions. Because of the problems associated with gambling, jobs are created in jails, prisons, hospitals, and private counseling offices around the country and world.

Addiction has a generic component to it that is genetic The genetic predisposition to addiction all starts with a choice, which ultimately destroys lives. Another friend talks as follows: I am a compulsive gambler choosing not to gamble. Further, the true addict in recovery knows that they can't just stop at one if they try it again. It is clear that while addiction is genetic, it is only the predisposition, and the addict makes an initial choice to try it.

An Open Letter from a Compulsive Gambler

Dear Readers,

I am writing to you in letter format to both apologize for my gambling and to give help to those who know a compulsive gambler that needs help.

As a compulsive gambler, I am acknowledging that my gambling may have influenced another person to start gambling. As a result of my gambling, I may have inflicted suffering on others who started because of my example and their family and friends to suffer just as those around me suffered. I know that there are those who were affected beyond my circle of influence, and while I cannot force someone to gamble, my actions could have encouraged it.

I also apologize to my ex-wife, sons, and family and friends who have had to put up with my absence and mood swings. My ex-wife and sons also have dealt with the worst possible consequences because of my gambling. My ex-wife lost financial security, and my sons lost opportunities to do things that they would have wanted to do. All the pain I caused my family can never be changed. It is my desire to change today and the future to cause no more harm. I hope that I can provide hope to those who are now dealing with addictive behavior.

I offer this advice to the gambler:

- Seek help before it gets too bad.
- Acknowledge that $1 lost is more than you can afford because once you start, it is hard to stop.
- Let family and friends know you need their help.

To the person dealing with a gambler:

- Look for ways to reach out to the gambler.
- Don't loan or help them financially.
- Be supportive of them if they are seeking help.
- If they don't acknowledge the problem, get other family and friends to help you with an intervention.
- If your state offers free or low cost counseling, seek it out for you and encourage the gambler to do likewise.

Finally, I give this hope: Help is available.

Check out these resources:

- Gamblers Anonymous
- Michigan Compulsive Gambling
- Never Enough

I sincerely hope to be of help to anyone who needs it.

Recovering With the help of God,

Thoughts and Reflections

Thoughts and Reflections

A NEW BEGINNING: 2012

So far, I have shared my prior writings on my addiction and the process of recovery, including what I felt was necessary as a part of my amends. As we go forward, I will talk more generally about compulsive gamblers in respect to the overall experiences and work on building a template of what could be a new future for recovery.

Compulsive gamblers have gone to the point of creating a new world where they continually chase the high of winning. The problem is that one win is not enough so they keep chasing it until they are broke and then they work on it with whatever means they can find. It is not always a financial "broke" that promotes the whatever-it takes mode as there are other losses that are destructive. I discussed them in the open letter. It becomes difficult to keep friends and relationships when the gambling takes the path of addiction.
Ask yourself: what would you do to escape problems? Oddly, that could become your personal addiction. With the compulsive gambler that is to some extent the case. Today I am in recovery and working on starting to rebuild what was lost. My losses were superficially financial but realistically far more severe. I lost my self respect, the people closest to me, and time that would have been with others. Toward the end, I missed time with my mother who died on January 17, 2007, just ten months before I went into recovery. What I would not do to change that and live some of it over to spend time with her. This is my new beginning!

Today, I have been working very hard at rebuilding relationships with my two sons and reevaluating what the future looks like. My desire is to see compulsive gambling treated as any other addiction would be and trying to catch the signs before the losses of life, relationships and money (purposely in that order) become too great to turn around. Today there are things that are private matters, but I keep very few secrets. I cannot afford to go back to where I was, so I have to plan a different path. The problem with that is that I have to keep my eyes open to other potential problems. Part of that is looking at fallacies that are a part of addiction and also a part of human nature.

Topics include the following:

☐ Id, Ego and, Super-Ego
- Gamblers Can Just Stop
- Sporadic Gambling Is Not Addicted Gambling

Other topics:

- Gambling Lies and Secrets
- Recovery
- Amends
- A Lifetime of Work
- Relapse
- Inevitable on Your Own
- The Need for Support
- Cross Addiction
- Co-Addictive Relationships
<u>Thoughts and Reflections</u>

Thoughts and Reflections

ID, EGO, AND SUPER-EGO

First let's make a chart:

Id = I want — no thought about right or wrong. Based on the Pleasure Principle.

Ego = How can I please the id while being realistic about it and avoiding the consequences? How can I balance what I (id) want with reality?

Super-ego = Very clearly opposes the id and actively infers right and wrong. Will oppose the ego when it leans too closely to the id.

Ultimately, the principle is that the ego is the mediator between the other two. The problem for addicts is that the 'I want' tends to win. Recovery is a lifelong journey to regain a balance. As such, it is necessary to look at the id and superego as the extremes. Neither of these can have an abundant control.

If for instance an addict feels down, the id might say, 'Let's just do it!' The super-ego says, 'No, that is not good.

Remember how much pain you had the last time?' The ego listens to both sides and says. 'How about this?' Translation... I want to gamble because life sucks right now... No way, you shouldn't do that. It is wrong, and the last time ... happened!

Well how about I go to a movie with friends?

Result — going to the movies with friends, which could be far better. Let's say that instead the id wins, and I go gamble. I start out feeling good, but by the end, it ends up the same as in the past, and I feel horrible now. For that matter, I feel worse in the end than when I started. Now what happens if the super-ego wins? I don't go gambling, and I don't do anything else either. I was down before, and I remain down. I might just sit there mulling over everything, and let's say the conclusion is I am an awful person. What happens now? I have heard it said that you want more id when in recovery and you are feeling down. I want the think-it-through process going on because there are other problems out there. Let's say it is not about gambling or a present addiction but rather about spending money on myself. Could the same problem end up being a part of the result? I.e. Could I become a spender and lose control of that? The answer is yes. I have the potential to become addicted to something else while in recovery from gambling, and undoubtedly, if I do not take the initiative to be aware of it I will find the substitute. There is plenty of evidence for 'cross addiction.' If you have been in a Casino or other venue where gambling is going on, what else do you see? How about this: Food, alcohol, and at one time, smoking. So, compulsive gamblers could also be over-eaters, alcoholics, or smokers. Oddly, compulsive gamblers may also be recovering from these addictions as well. I have heard people in recovery from other addictions discount gambling as a possible problem. However, almost no compulsive gambler will discount the crossing over to another addiction. The topic of 'cross addiction' will be discussed in detail later. However the id, ego, and super-ego thought process needs to be realized before getting there.

Since addiction is often an issue of controlling a desire for a high, there is a natural draw to find a substitute high that was and is my curse in recovery. I need to be aware of that desire for a high to avoid it with a new addiction. Are there things that are desirable and make you feel good that could distract you from other interactions? Even now, I urge people to become aware of these hidden draws.

<u>Thoughts and Reflections</u>

Thoughts and Reflections

Thoughts and Reflections

GAMBLERS CAN JUST STOP!!

Most recovering compulsive gamblers have heard that phrase. People think that we can just stop but do not think the same of over eaters, alcoholics, or most other addictions. Let's say you love reading books, and you find one that is very compelling. People say that it is so good they just 'can't put it down.' Can you think of something that is so compelling or enjoyable that you get lost in it, and time gets away from you? The compulsive gambler is in that place. Often, they can't stop until the money runs out (until the end). In recovery, the compulsive gambler is fighting a desire that for them is as necessary as breathing. If it is looked at like that, can you just stop breathing? The only difference between breathing and addiction is that breathing is necessary and the addiction is believed to be necessary for the addict. In the case of compulsive gambling, even when the person becomes aware, it can still be hard to quit. I went to my first meeting and heard stories of what losses others had experienced and proceeded to buy a lottery ticket when I left the meeting. I consider that moment a life saver because I immediately broke down and realized I could not continue on the path I was on.

A compulsive gambler seldom talks about the losses and almost always talks about the wins. It is part of the illusion that has to be supported to keep doing what they are doing. The worst part is that as I stated earlier with my open letter, it brings others into the fantasy and expands the wake of destruction. Have you ever watched someone gambling and seen them win? How about losing? Do the promoters of gambling ever have a commercial showing someone losing to promote the business? Would that make you go there? The answers are obvious. At least they should be to anyone who desires to be free of addiction or knows someone with an addiction.

How about this for a comparison? Weight Loss programs tell about the people who are successful but not so much about the failures. If the success story ends up gaining the weight back, who do you hear it from? People do not like to admit failure or relapse. The programs are not eager to tell about them because that would discredit them.

If you lost weight on a program, you have a success story everyone wants to hear, but when you gain it back, do they want to hear it? Does the weight gain get reported, and if it does, is it accredited to the program or to the failure of the individual?

There is sporadic success and failure. Does this change the fact that the person is overweight?

Thoughts and Reflections

<u>Thoughts and Reflections</u>

SPORADIC GAMBLING IS NOT ADDICTED GAMBLING

While working on recovery, I have heard a term used that is to me very silly: Harm Reduction. It means being able to gamble with limits. It is a belief that someone can learn to control the urge to gamble to the point of reasonable limits. Consider this: is this possible with alcoholics, drug addicts, or smokers to stop at a safe point?

I agree with someone I met in recovery who said, "why stop at one?' You can't get the high with one lottery ticket, one drink, one cigarette, or one pill so what is the point? If someone goes out to eat can they fill up with one fry, onion ring, or other appetizer? No, they go there to get a meal not a single item. They don't go there, order a single piece of appetizer, and then leave. Why would anyone stop before they get the 'buzz' or 'high' that they have become accustomed to? Why would someone take one bite of a burger? They won't be full, which is why they bought the burger.

I started off with a scratch-off ticket every now and then. It did not go to the extreme from the beginning. Just like with other addictions, it started out slow, and as time went on, it took more to get the same feeling. At the end, it did not matter how much I gambled. I could not get to the same point. My point is that it started out just for fun and random and ended up over the top.

So much of compulsive gambling is hidden until it is too late because it is not usually recognized as a problem. It is clearly acceptable and is growing in popularity on so many levels. The governmental agencies enjoy huge tax gains, so they are not likely to stop. There is a part of the government conscience that makes sure there is help out there for those who want help, but generally speaking, it is not strong enough to say no way. In the United States, there are only two states that do not have legalized gambling (Hawaii and Utah). In the 1970's, only two states had legalized gambling, and oddly, it all started in Nevada because of the Great Depression. As financial recovery for Nevada was spurred by it over the last thirty years of the 20th century, other states began to take notes from Nevada and then New Jersey.

The point to this is that compulsive gamblers could not be gambling regularly in the early years because it took more travel or was limited by accessibility. As time has passed, accessibility has increased and thus the frequency and acceptability has also become more the norm. Just as alcoholism has always been there (even during prohibition), so compulsive gambling has always been there. The more acceptable it became, the more visible it became. Amazingly, as gambling began to show signs of helping economic growth, the state governments saw it as an income stream. The problem to consider is at what cost? Financial destruction of compulsive gamblers, crime rates, and tax evasion? The destructive forces will be discussed in my next section. For now, I want to talk about sporadic or occasional gamblers. These are the once a month or 'special event' gamblers, and I would propose that many have a problem as well.

Today there are multiple ways to gamble, and there are people who have a favorite form, but I also know that gambling is gambling no matter what form it takes. If a person gambles at the casino once in a while, they are at risk. That risk goes up if between these times, they 'occasionally' gamble in one or more other ways. The other ways include sports betting, state lotteries, bingo, family or friends poker nights, or any other form imaginable. The problem is that I can't say what the other forms might be because there are forms of gambling that are a matter of individual design. What I am referring to are ways that mimic what I talked about from my youth: Competitions that may not have any money involved such as drinking, eating, or any other form of compulsive competitions. So let's say an individual goes to the casino because it's fun occasionally, and between those visits, they buy scratch-off tickets occasionally. Then let's say between those scratch offs, they play bingo and/ or private poker games. There is a high probability that the person has a problem, but the call has to be by the individual as no one can convince gamblers they have a problem until they get to a bottom that is personal. The hardest thing to do is to find a compulsive gambler if they don't want to be found. Other forms of addiction are seen because of the effects of the ingested substance. However, a compulsive gambler has signs that do not raise the same red flags. They are seen in the lies and secrets in the gamblers life, both their own and those of the people around them.

Thoughts and Reflections

Thoughts and Reflections

Thoughts and Reflections

GAMBLING LIES AND SECRETS

The world is full of lies and secrets: a sad truth but more so for compulsive gamblers and those around them. The compulsive gambler has a web of lies that support the fantasies and hide the problem. They have secrets that allow them to hide what is behind the fantasy. Just as bad is that the people in the gambler's life often build their own lies and secrets to protect themselves from the gambler in their life and/ or their own problem gambling.

The first clear lie for a compulsive gambler is "I do not have a problem, and I can quit at any time." At the time of my writing this book, this is still the view of most judges, probation officers, and a majority of the people who encounter the compulsive gambler. While there are many people who can stop at will, there are others who, like alcoholics, cannot stop so easily. The problem is that many compulsive gamblers have other coexisting addictions or have recovered from one addiction only to find gambling as a substitute.

Many people I have met have had other addictions and or mental health issues before the gambling. I can honestly say that I am no exception to that. Over the years, I tried smoking, drinking, and a few other similar addictions, which never really worked for me. There were some that worked well though, including but not limited to eating, Mountain Dew, and chocolate. I also have the diagnoses of ADHD and BiPolar with the main focus on long-term depression. This being said the mental health diagnoses are not the main focus in this, and I will address many of the lies and secrets from a purely addiction perspective.

Here are some other lies of the compulsive gambler:

1. I am doing this to make life better for others.
2. I have a system.
3. I am a winner.
4. I'll win my losses back.
5. I don't need to stop.
6. I can gamble just a little.
7. What I am doing is not gambling.
8. I'm not like the losers.
9. I can pay back what I owe.
10. My family will understand why I am not able to be there for...

As I said, there are lies related to those around the compulsive gambler too. Some of those are:

1. He/She works hard. They deserve an outlet.
2. He/She is not that bad.
3. We have fun when we are there together.
4. I like all the comps.
5. There is nothing wrong with having a little fun.

Both the compulsive gambler and those around them have a vested interest in living with these lies. Part of it is that they believe them, and part is that to accept the truth makes the whole world crash down around them. As I had said earlier, no one goes into their adult life and says, "Oh I'll bury myself in debt" or "It would be fun to be broke." These lies are without a doubt the path to that kind of statement. In my experience, some gamblers have people close to them who are unwittingly enablers by living their own secret lies.

As a compulsive gambler, I can say that when it all starts, there is a misconception that you will win and do wonderful things with those winnings. My vision was that my family would have everything they needed, that I would be able to help my church and give to causes for a long time to come. I also dreamed of traveling without worry where ever I wanted and whenever I wanted.

I remember my system when I started, and in the end, all I wanted to do was gamble. The system did not matter anymore. So, what was my system? I worked in a convenience store, which is the perfect job for a scratch-off gambler because after work, I'd start gambling. While working, I would watch to see what others bought and how long it has been since a winner or how many winners have been returned. I believed that I could get the winner during the time I was playing after work most of the time by what I thought was "playing the House." Unlike others, I was able to see what was bought, what was won, and what was lost throughout the day. At the end of the day, I had seen where the winners were likely to be. Sadly it seldom, if ever, worked, but I still believed in my "system." I believed it so much that I was gambling more and more as time went on. I became so tied into it that I believed that I was ahead and winning

The lie that "I am a winner" became my personal hidden belief. I look back and realize that I was losing and losing a lot. The problem back when I was at the peak of my gambling is that I blocked out the loosing and only looked at what I won. My reality was not about the money by the end, and I point to the fact that when someone asked me about it, I could never say how much I had won or lost. So by the end, I would talk about my winning while scratching off tickets at the store in a small area where customers sat. Looking back, I can't believe that I believed the lie and shared that lie with others at the store. Because I had some level of realization that I was losing it became clear that I had to set up a subconscious lie to myself to allow me to feel better about the losses. So because I was a winner I convinced myself that I would get ahead again. Thus my rationalizing the losses became "I'll win it all back." Winning back my losses became the rational for spending more and continually finding the money to use to win it back. For me, it was always in my mind to remember that "The next one would be the winner." These lies were important to keep me living in the fantasy. They set up the belief that helped avoid the reality that I was a compulsive gambler.

I became focused on winning it back and vested on getting the resources to do that at any cost. It led to the desire to keep going and believe falsely that I did not need to stop. Why would I stop? I believed I was on the verge of winning it all back, and even more importantly, I was going to win a lot more. As I grew weary of the chase for money I grew to enjoy the chase for the sake of the chase. At that point I began to believe that it was ok to gamble a little so then it promoted a new lie for me.

> I believed that I could gamble "just a little bit." It is easy to keep going when I convinced myself that I was gambling just a little. Hey I believed that gambling every day after work for one or two hours was just a little bit, so it was ok. Sadly, that is how I was gambling most of the time anyway, so I really did not have a problem... Right? Wrong! I needed to justify my escape somehow, and I enjoyed this form of escaping the best.

I felt it was harmless and actually helpful in problem resolution for me.

That means that I was not gambling, I was just winding down after work. I was able to get away from my problems and "work" on a resolution to them in my own eyes. My view that I was just winding down after work and not really gambling was an illusion that made my gambling more dangerous because it opens me to lies to myself. It moved me to the next part of my world.

I am not like all those other gamblers…"I am not like the losers." What a mess that lie was because I got **slapped** into reality after my first GA meeting on this lie. Earlier, I mentioned how I went to my first meeting, heard all these real stories of losses, left the meeting telling myself the lie, and when I bought a scratch-off ticket five minutes later, I came to reality. For about two years, I watched others come to the store I worked at and spend money on the lottery and told myself I was not like them. I watched them buy "numbers" and scratch-offs all the time, thinking that they were losing so much money, and my system was superior to what they were doing. The lie behind it was that I believed I was not like them. My realization was that I was exactly like those other gamblers and, in some cases, worse. Not all of the people I watched gamble were regular gamblers. This leads into the lie that I can pay back what I owe.

Remember that compulsive gambling is not all financial in nature, so not everything I owed was the financial. During my time of compulsive gambling, I was absent from my sons' lives at times. How does a person pay back not being there at times? Whatever I do, I will never be able to give back the time missed because it has passed. Compulsive gamblers have no way to go back and play with one of their children when they were five. Once the child is six I cannot go back in time and spend time with them when they were five. Compulsive gamblers lose these special moments. If they look at relationships with family, friends, and significant others, how does anyone get time back to spend it with these other people when you were gambling? The bottom line of believing they can pay back what they owe is that it focuses on the money and denies the other costs that cannot be recovered because they are not borrowing the time that never can be recovered. The final lie to look at for the compulsive gambler is that those close to them will understand their absence while they are gone. The compulsive gambler, however, does not tell family and friends that they are gambling but rather make it sound like they are out working or some other activity. Often this is the hardest to cover up. It is hard to keep the lies straight and as a result, explaining inconsistencies, which show up at times and at the end when it all comes unraveled. The problem is that often there is someone in the compulsive gamblers life that is an enabler, and they often have their own lies to protect.

If the enabler is supportive of the gambler, their lies might start with "They are hard workers, and they need an outlet." That plays into the belief that they don't have that bad of a problem, so it's not a problem, which plays into the idea that when they go together, it is fun. These lies are a slippery slope for an enabling person.

This person may begin to enjoy the 'comps.' For those who don't know what 'comps' are, they are specials for 'high rollers.' If you are spending enough at the Casinos, they will send you 'free' nights, meals, house money, and other items to bring you back. Because the Casino has made a lot off the high roller, they make these available to them. In reality, compulsive gamblers have paid for these comps or are losing enough that they will. These 'comps' lead to an enabler beginning to overlook the flaws in the lies and grab onto one that is even grander. They build the self-justifying lie that there is nothing wrong with having a little fun (focused on gambling as the fun).

These lies are all foundational to the secrets held by the compulsive gambler and to those who are a part of their lives. The problem is that these secrets are not ones that are general in nature. They are individualized to the gambler's life and to the lives of those around them. Some of them may be shared, and some of them are personal. At this point, I can only address my own as they are ones I own as part of my recovery.

I will list a few of them but not all of them because of all the territory yet to cover and the secrets are better covered by the individual over time. Here are five of my secrets, or at least, I believed them to be secret.

1. I never believed that I was able to become addicted because when I started smoking. It was not a positive experience. I have gone back to it now and then, but because it affected my breathing negatively, I quit quickly.

2. I never considered compulsive behavior an addiction until my experience in recovery from gambling.

3. Because I watched my mother-in-law gamble, and I had seen others do it, I could not recognize it as an addiction.

4. I really believed I could avoid my problems by not addressing them with the person I felt drove me there.

5. I desired to be better than I was and struggled to meet what I believed would make my ex-wife happier.

These are hard to explain because they focus on self-image and what were personal perceptions for me. So I will move on, leaving you to think about the topic of secrets as you may find secrets that are not really secrets to those close to the addict. I do not want to plant ideas any further on the secrets aspect because for you it will help keep them personal.

Thoughts and Reflections

Thoughts and Reflections

<u>RECOVERY</u>

This is the road less traveled because an addict has a hard time finding it on their own, yet it cannot be forced upon them. It took me being suicidal to find the road to recovery. At that point, life is almost completely destroyed. Addicts have had court orders for treatment when it comes to substances but seldom if ever is it recommended for compulsive gamblers. Most compulsive gamblers lose the freedom noted by prison sentences when they are caught in schemes to get the needed money once the legitimate sources dry up. Others have committed suicide, and unless a person left clear connections to the gambling, it may not be linked. This can be seen by news reports of people who die at a casino or other place where they leave apology letters. Those who find the road to recovery have had a personal discovery or been at a point where they are found out by others and are guided to the path.

I found recovery through the threat of job loss followed by a family revelation and then a stay in an adult psych. unit. Once I left, I could have returned to my addiction, but thanks to GA and the fellowship there, I became aware of my addiction in a way that was irrefutable for me. Earlier, I told the story of my last bet after my first meeting, which is the final proof for me. Here is the longer version of it.

In late 2007, I was buying scratch-off tickets to avoid going home to my ex-wife because finances were a problem and led to arguments. Since I often worked shifts that were opposite of my ex, it was easy to make an excuse to avoid being there when she was awake or home. At some point, I was given three days pending, and while I was able to get my job back, there were consequences. I realized that I needed to explain something to my ex-wife. I did some of that but still kept secrets that put me on path to suicidal depression. The results were that I ended up being admitted to the psych unit for the depression and my ex-wife was able to look at stuff I had on my car and at the house without my interference, which led her to discover more about my gambling problem.

This made my depression worse and brought me home to an angry wife ultimately. Upon release from the hospital, I was told I needed to get help. That help was in many forms, but ultimately, the biggest help came from the table of a GA meeting.

This is where I heard stories of losses, and took the twenty question test and passed it. After passing it with flying colors, hearing stories of the destruction brought on by the addiction, and then went on to blow my cover story that I was not that bad. I did that by driving out of the parking lot and to my favorite place to get gas where I bought a one dollar scratchoff ticket. This was unconscionable for me because I lost the ability to deny I had a problem in my eyes.

I have to believe that recovery is a process that starts because of the addict's lack of support for their unrealistic fantasy. Every addict has a different bubble burst in order to go into recovery and recovery never ends, it continues for life.

In time, the addict needs to begin working on making amends.

This is the move that begins with themselves because they can't forgive others without forgiving themselves.

Thoughts and Reflections

Thoughts and Reflections

<u>AMENDS</u>

There is a process to the amends that for me had to begin in my own 'skin.' I reached the point of wanting to die in order to avoid facing my disastrous results both for me and for those I affected. My earlier 'Open Letter' was because I realized that the worst destruction that was caused by my gambling were those who I affected without having ever met or been aware of. Imagine how hard it would be if you were a compulsive gambler, and you became a role model for others who would take on the addiction. Unlike other addictions, which are seen as addictions, compulsive gambling is not seen as a problem by most because of how 'helpful' it is for local economies and government entities.

Compulsive gamblers find themselves in a position exactly as any other addict when they reach the point of recovery with the exception that when it all ends, there is a lack of understanding of how they got there. People see the staggering alcoholic and the glassy eyed drug addict, but the compulsive gambler is not noticed until disaster hits. Making amends is difficult because almost no amount of change is acceptable, and it is not easy to get past what happened. Courts and non-gamblers will often say you could have just stopped. People may ask questions like:

- How could you spend that much?
- Don't you love your family?
- What is wrong with you?
- How could you be so blind to how much you spent?

- How could you miss...? Your...was so disappointed

- Don't you care that we have lost the house?

For compulsive gamblers, these are the questions that need answers for significant others but mostly for themselves. Until the end, I never realized just how bad things were. When I started recovery, I had to find a way to stop the cycle that, years before, I said I would never do. I remembered the promise to myself, and it was as if I had failed twice by doing one thing. I told myself I would never do what I was doing, and I did it to the extent that I had caused myself to destroy everything around me. Sometimes amends cannot be done because they will be hurt as much or more by the realization of what was done. Amends are less about the past and more about the present and the future. Amends are necessary as much for the addict as for those who were caught in the destructive wake. Many of the amends I did were not accepted as enough, or for the person, they were not the amends they wanted. These amends are for any person who was affected by the compulsive gambler's actions. Some, however, as I mentioned above are people you never met. Even though amends are actively done, they are not always accepted and often the process lasts a lifetime.

Thoughts and Reflections

Thoughts and Reflections

A LIFETIME OF WORK

Compulsive gamblers have not gotten where they are overnight, and they are not going to recover overnight. No matter how long it took to get to the point of beginning the process of recovery, the addict will have a lifetime of work to stay in recovery. The biggest problem with recovery is that even staying away from the addiction does not mean they will stay clean. Staying away from our original addiction is only part of the process. An addict needs to be vigilant all of their life because of cross addiction. It is not uncommon to recover from one addiction and just when everything seems to be better to pick up a new one. If you or someone you know is recovering from compulsive gambling, beware of that which becomes too fun or that seems to be taking hold of you. Because of my awareness, here is what I believe is my list of addictions I have had personal experience with over the years.

- Eating
- Smoking
- Pop Drinking
- Shopping
- Computer
- Gambling

This is by no means a complete list of the possible addictions in my past and not all of them are done for me. I still spend a lot of time on the internet, eating and shopping at times. The hardest part of recovery for me is recognizing that I will never be done recovering. It is also hard to maintain certain activities that I need to keep doing and assessing if I am doing too much or if it is reasonable. Each day is truly the first day of recovery for me because I know if I stop believing that the problem is there, I take the chance of relapse.

Recovery is a lifetime job for any addict. There are problems with the gambling addict in that there are a lot of different ways to gamble and not all of them are accepted by compulsive gamblers as such. This means that relapse is much more probable. Those who have relapsed have the ability to keep it secret even from their fellow addicts because it is harder to see the signs.

Thoughts and Reflections

<u>Thoughts and Reflections</u>

<u>RELAPSE</u>

Here we are at a place where two truths are going to be addressed:
That it is almost impossible to recover on your own and that without any support, it is inevitable that you will relapse. On my own, I headed into my addiction without hesitation to my own destruction. Without any core support outside of myself it would be senseless to stop because it brought me a 'buzz.' If you are enjoying a piece of chocolate, and you have a whole candy bar are you going to stop at one bite? Most people would not stop at that one bite. Why? Because unless you have others who are there either to share it with or to set the limit of one bite, it makes no sense to you. There are people who can stop at one beer but on average since one beer does nothing for people they would not stop. It makes no sense to stop at one or two when it takes more than that to get the 'buzz' or feel you have achieved the effect you want. The value of having others to be accountable to is that they will help you look at your addiction differently. I again refer back to my attendance at my first GA meeting. I heard the stories, but until I accepted my problem, it was not real to me. When in recovery, a support system is absolutely necessary because an addict does not get to the bottom without a support system. Compulsive gamblers have other gamblers and or suppliers of the environment. In recovery, I realized how much I created a system that supported my compulsive gambling, so in order to have success in recovery, I need to surround myself with a support system as well.

The gambler's support system is a false one, so in recovery, they need a real one. That real one has to be composed of people who want them to get better. This is sometimes difficult because many of the people in their circle are from three central groups. The first are the promoters of the various forms of gambling. Next are other compulsive gamblers and lastly are people caught in the wake of the gamblers destruction. As a result, compulsive gamblers have a lot of problems building that support system. Some of this support system is completely out and others depend on the forgiveness factor.

Family members can be a great support. However, many compulsive gamblers have done the greatest harm to those people closest to them. Some hold out hope for their loved ones and become a part of the support system in recovery and others loose hope and need space. The compulsive gambler has a lot of work to do in recovery that is totally theirs to do. Part of that is figuring out the support system that is going to work best for them.

This all comes down to the desire of the compulsive gambler to surround themselves with people who are invested in recovery or to surround themselves with people who have different goals in mind. Clearly if you surround yourself with those who are stuck in the gambling world then that is the path you will follow. So the compulsive gambler fights for recovery, with the desire to return to their addiction ever present, as they look for their higher power in the will of their support system.

Without a support system, relapse is inevitable. Without the support of others, relapse is as likely to me as a compulsive eater in recovery at an all you can eat buffet. There is a problem that can crop up if you are not careful during recovery it is called cross addiction.

Thoughts and Reflections

Thoughts and Reflections

CROSS-ADDICTION

Cross addiction is what happens when an addict is in recovery and becomes addicted to something new. It is not always accepted by an addict that when they quit one addiction, they can end up with another, but realistically, if an addict does not accept the possibility of cross addiction, it is almost as inevitable as relapse. During the time compulsive gamblers are gambling, they may also be drinking alcohol, smoking, or over eating. So what happens is that as they recover from the compulsive gambling these other co-existing addictions tend to fill in the gaps. Often, it is either not noticed or some of the same false beliefs that supported a previous addiction begin to strengthen the new addiction.

As I stated earlier, there is a genetic predisposition for addiction, but it is my belief that it is generic in nature (a predisposition to addiction without a specific addiction). That is why I encourage compulsive gamblers to be aware of the potential for some new addiction to take them back down the path that they have traveled before. It is necessary for me to point out that the path may seem different, but the end result is the same as sure as the Earth revolves around the Sun. It is up to you where you go in your recovery and when you plan the route, be willing to accept route changes as needed to avoid going the same places even though the road is a new one.

Thoughts and Reflections

CO-ADDICTIVE RELATIONSHIPS

Co-addictive relationships can range from the couple who gambles together to two people who feed off the problems as a way to feel better about themselves. There are many types of co-addictive relationships, and each person has to look into this on his or her own to find them. I will attempt to list some of them from my perspective and experience but want to point out that this is from my own view.

Here is a list to start with:

- Co-Dependent Co-Addiction
- Dual Co-Addicted.
- Blind Addicted Enablers
- Enabling Addiction
- Double Blind Addiction
- Denial Addiction
- Openly Aware Addiction Supportive

Co-dependent co-addiction is a relationship where one person is focused on a relationship of total dependency to each other and the other is dependent on the addiction to cope with being co-dependent. In other words each person is dependent on the other and they are addicted to this codependent relationship as much to their chosen addiction.

Dual co-addicted - Two people who both enjoy the same addiction and do it together. It would seem this is the hardest situation to get into recovery because often the relationship has some basis in the addiction as the attraction.

Blind = Enablers - A person who enables the addict by not seeing it. They tend to not want to see it for fear of what they might find out. The addict is eager to please that denial because they don't see what they are doing as a problem.

Enabling Addiction - The enabler in this relationship is fully aware of the addiction and may even be a supplier to help promote the addiction.

Double Blind Addiction – This is the case of two people who are both in the addiction and neither of them sees it as a problem.

Denial Addiction – One person is aware of the addiction but denies it exists. The other simply enjoys the addiction but does not believe it is an addiction.

Openly Aware Addiction Supportive - Both people in this relationship are aware of the addiction and could care less to avoid it. The addiction is a part of the relationship like going to dinner. No one is ready to change, and for this relationship, the only way anything is going to change is if there is a major disaster related to the problem.

Thoughts and Reflections

Thoughts and Reflections

FINAL POINTS AND A SUMMARY OF MY RECOVERY TODAY

At this point I want to talk about how compulsive gamblers might attempt to hide the financial and other problems as they became more obvious to those around them. Below is a list of possible things that might be done. These are not meant to be hurtful and may be done by others who are not gamblers with a problem.

1. Intercepting the mail.

2. Shredding bills and collection notices.

3. Failing to answer their cell phones while in the throes of their gambling.

4. Talking about their big wins but being silent when they lost.

5. Taking extra cash with them, so they can claim to have won it if asked.

6. Shuffle money in accounts.

7. If they have access to funds, there is the possibility of 'borrowing" money with the intention of paying it back before it is noticed, which may lead to being charged with criminal actions such as embezzlement, theft, and/or perjury.

8. If it gets bad enough, they might attempt suicide to get out of the problems.

9. Different types of crimes of desperation, which under normal situations would never be considered by the person.

10. Lying about where they are and missing work as a result.

The best way to learn about the person is to help them get help. This list is small and leaves room for other things. Sadly not everyone gets to experience their bottom the same way. Unlike other addictions, the symptoms are not always going to be visible to those around them.

My bottom was explained earlier in this book. Sadly the losses that were the hardest for me were ones people don't often realize are there. I am blessed that I have two sons and a number of family members that I believed I had lost that are still a part of my life.

So now I leave it up to you to decide if you believe in the addiction of Compulsive Gambling. This leaves you two choices.

1. Deny the existence of the addiction and do nothing.
2. Believe the existence of compulsive gambling and help others understand that it exists.

Thoughts and Reflections

Thoughts and Reflections

Thoughts and Reflections

30 DAY DETOX FOR GAMBLERS

30 days to Detox for Gamblers

Before you begin I am asking you to consider the pattern of addiction. Ask yourself these questions and ponder your answers along with reading the poem on the next page for your first day.

How often do you say you can stop? *Everyday, until I start then I lose control.*

Have you ever told someone that you don't have a problem? *yes.*

Do you believe you have a problem? *yes.*

A Variation on: Autobiography In Five Short Chapters

1.

I head toward my addiction.
The addiction is a deep hole
I fall into it.
I am lost... I feel helpless.
I blame others.
It takes forever to escape it.

2.

I head toward the addiction again.
The addiction is still a deep hole.
I pretend it does not exist.
I fall into it again.
I can't believe I am back in the
hole but, I still blame
others.
It again takes forever to escape.

3.

I head toward the addiction again.
I see the deep hole of Addiction.
I pretend it is not there
I still fall in ...it is a patterned
habit.
I see it clearly
I know this place.
I take responsibility for it.
I escape immediately.

4.

I head toward the addiction
again. I see the deep hole of
addiction I avoid it at the
last second.

5.

I change my path avoiding the addiction entirely

Day one is all about deciding that you have a problem and that you need help. Your success depends on that premise. If someone has ordered you to get help and you are not interested in help it just will not happen. You can't do it for anyone else. Life is better in recovery but it is not a cake walk.

With Compulsive Gambling, for the sake of argument, let's consider the 'ingested substances' as the following:

- The act of Gambling
- The Feelings Gambling provide
- The 'environment' of gambling o Lights o Sounds
  o Smells
    o People
- The things that you may be avoiding o Arguments o Problems o Low self esteem
  o Depression

What we are going to do with this 'Detox' is work on changing the thought process and focus on daily assignments. We are going to work on focusing on a thought each day. Here is the process I am suggesting for those in the first days of recovery. In doing this hopefully you will find a path that is hidden from you while you are in your addiction.

The first day is to use those questions above to evaluate your own perspective on the problem.

Each day you should write your thoughts relative to the thought you are focusing on. Treat it as a medication that is needed to fight a disease, because addiction is a disease. Compulsive Gambling is a disease that often is missed until the damage is very severe, few if any signs are there like with alcohol and other ingested substances.

So:

- Day 1 is the self-assessment process.
  - Ask yourself the 3 questions. o Read the poem and consider how you fit into that cycle.
  - Write down at least one or two sentences about your thoughts. Do it at least two times a day.
- Day 2: Focus on the Poem and write down thoughts at least twice during the day.
- Day 3: Repeat days 1 and 2 together.
- Day 4 through 30: Pick a new thought for the day from the book and think about how it applies to you.
  - Write down your thoughts at least 2 times a day.
    - Focus on those thoughts and what you are writing.
    - If you want or feel the urge write more than the 2 times a day.

As I stated this process is meant to try and 'detox' your thoughts and allow you to make it through those early days.

Here is why I am suggesting this. I am a compulsive Gambler and my last bet was November 21, 2007. That is also the date of my first meeting. I allowed myself to think I did not have a problem and immediately after the meeting I bought a scratch off ticket. That moment was my water shed moment. I swore I would find a way to stop.

My first thought after buying that ticket was I need to find a different focus. Since that first meeting I have continued to attend Gamblers Anonymous as best I could.

This was hard because in the beginning of my recovery I was thinking about gambling continuously. Until I decided I was going to do exactly what I am suggesting to you here. I still struggle, BUT each morning I think of a simple saying to focus on and that in combination with meetings has kept me focused. I only wrote this because of some friends who have voiced their struggles to get through those first days and months.

At the Back of this Book you will find one page for each day from 4 through 30 to use as your journaling area if you choose to do so. This is so you can chose which Thought for the day you want rather than a specific order for them. You may want to write down the thought you chose at the top of each page.

Day One:

Day Two:

<u>Day Three:</u>

Together We Can

"Just because I can't do it alone doesn't make me weak."
Bernard Zeitler

Well I realized that my first 'Thought for Today" was a repeat of yesterday. It still applies but I try not to repeat the same thing 2 days in a row. When I come to an awareness of the thought I want to share it is often because of reading someone who shared their experiences.

The Thought for Today series I started because of a desire to have my mind on something that is encouraging and to share those thoughts with others who are struggling. I couldn't do it without others. But as the thought I am sharing says, I'm not weak because I need others to inspire me. It is precisely the fact that I need others that makes me strong. Remember: in weakness we are strong.

A Thought For Today

"When you've lost everything you didn't know you had recovery finds you."

Bernard Zeitler

In the above picture there are two bikes. The one in the foreground was restored by my father and I. Behind it is the one we did not restore. Both were the same when bought in the early 1950's and over time they both decayed sitting in a barn. They were both a mess when my dad and I started working on the one in the foreground. That was in 2010, the summer before he died.

Until we worked on that bike we had no idea what we had lost, but in restoring it we not only restored the bike but our relationship was mended. It was part of my amends as I recovered from Compulsive Gambling.

My addiction had taken so much from me and it was not until I started recovery that I could see what I lost.

What situation has been interfering with relationships that you were not aware of until recently? Is there a situation that interferes with something in your life?

"Patience is Recovery in the moment of an urge. It is better to put a penny in the slot of a piggy bank than a machine in that moment."
Bernard Zeitler

Have you ever had an urge to eat a piece of chocolate or any favorite food? How about to do a favorite activity?

I have heard and seen over time how my compulsive gambling and other activities have driven me when I allow the 'urge' control the 'moment'. It seldom ends up being as good as I thought it would be. When it did, it did not last. Some days there is an urge to get things done faster than they should be done, but I've learned to allow myself to be in the moment rather than in the urge. What challenges do you experience when the urge collides with the moment you are in?

Toilet Paper And Life

"Life is like a roll of toilet paper. You are constantly rolling along with the potential to be flushed." Bernard Zeitler

Have you ever thought about how Life is constantly changing? Life continually 'rolls' out new experiences and it we are not prepared we can have troubles that will 'flush' our hopes.

Last night I was feeling a bit down and realized that change, even when you want it has an effect on your perspective. It is often very difficult to realize that as life 'rolls' along the past is gone and our future is still hidden in the 'roll'. All we have is now and yet we need to prepare for the future enough to know we are not at a loss. How are you at letting life roll out before you and letting the past go so that you are ready for the present.. What is your thoughts on life and the comparison of Toilet Paper?

Recovery Is Not A One Time Thing

"Recovery is time sensitive, every moment matters."
Bernard Zeitler

In life we realize that time is a fluid and changing. As a child we depend on others to care for us. As adults we learn to take care of ourselves and children (if we have them). But there is a time when we grow older and again depend on others. Depending on health issues that dependence may be different, but it is still there.

Can we accept that our life is a matter of living each moment as if it were the most important one we have? Can we see that every moment is a process of recovering from the moment that came before it? How are you 'living in this moment'?

Temptation And Time In Addiction

"Discouragement is temporary, recovery is in the moment and long term."

Bernard Zeitler

Often in a moment of distress a person gravitates toward their addiction. In that moment it is important to focus on why we are in recovery. Doing that often will help hold the moment and make it through even if only 'by the skin of our teeth'. In so doing we survive for the long term as opposed to fall into the temporary solution that only makes things worse.

What is that fallback position for you when you become discouraged? Is it:

Chocolate

Pop/Soda

Food

Gambling

Dispute

Sleep

How do you remember the moment?

Over Confidence

"If you can live without air then you can gamble without losing."
Bernard Zeitler

As a child there was a practice of holding your breath until you got what you wanted. The problem is that we lose consciousness if we hold it too long. It seldom if ever was successful. As adults we have some things we hold onto until it hurts without realizing that we are 'holding our breath' to get what we want.

If we go to an 'all you can eat restaurant' do we feel the need to eat more so we 'get our monies worth'? There are plenty of people who do indeed do that. The same thing happens with addiction.

As a compulsive gambler, I was intent on keeping the action going until I 'made my money back' or 'won big'. It was a false hope that took disaster to break.
Remember the idea that we need to breathe more than we 'need' those things that prevent us from living a good life.

What Hurts More?

"Believing a lie doesn't make it true and denying the truth only hurts your own life."
Bernard Zeitler

How often do we tell ourselves that something is not as bad as it is? Above is the car I was driving in 2013 when someone decided to run a stop sign. I should not have been able to walk away but I did.

When a person is not facing their own biases and problems it really hurts them. My Gambling was hidden from others, or so I thought and until I faced the problem I could not make progress.

What are you hiding from? How are you facing a problem in your life?

It's Not About How Long.

"Be proud of this moment clean, not in the amount of time clean. This moment is the one that matters most right now." Bernard Zeitler

I am a Compulsive Gambler in Recovery. An addict who is 'clean' right now. so which is more important? That I have been 'clean' since November 21, 2007 or that I am clean right now?

There is a riddle about which came first... The Chicken or the egg. Does it really matter today? We have both and can enjoy the chicken as a meal and the egg as a meal. People eat both but does it matter to you when you are hungry which came first?

In my recovery I know when my last bet was but it does not change that I gambled in the past or that I am not gambling now. What matters to me and to those who love me is that I am not gambling right now. I've heard people get upset about a relapse after having been 'clean' for days, weeks, months and years. I can't change that, but I can change right now. Right now I have decided in this moment to be 'clean' I can't worry about what might happen or what has already happened. So here is my key to having been clean for years: It only matters that I am not gambling right now. When the anniversaries come I will celebrate them but I will remain focused on right now because it is all that I can control.

How about you? Are there things you have milestones that you celebrate that you focus on without thinking about the moment you are in?

Living An Illusion

"Believing a lie doesn't make it true and denying the truth only hurts your own life."
Bernard Zeitler

In life what we see is not always what is real. Have you ever heard or saw something that you believed without question only to find out it wasn't what it appeared?

In addiction this is common because it is the 'lie' that seems real for a time. In politics this 'illusion' is used to get votes. We are offered something for nothing often after the electlin it isn't there. In life if we believe something and think it is true only to find it to be a lie it hurts. How do you deal with the truth when t is not what you 'want' it to be?

Words And Actions

"Your words may say one thing but are your actions in agreement?"
Bernard Zeitler

Often we hear people making promises, telling what they believe and discussing their day. The question came to me: Is it synchronized? Do the words and actions fit?

Jesus addressed this regularly.

1. He overturned tables in the synagogue when money changers and salesment were corrupting it.
2, A group of men brought an adultress to him for stoning and he reminded them of their sins.
3. The diciples said things and were reminded of what it meant.

When we get so confident that we say something without acting in a way that is consistent with it our words fall silent. I try to remember what my actions should be when I say something, but sometimes I forget that connection. How are you doing with this?

Accidents Are Not Always As Bad As They Appear

"What we think is true doesn't make it true."
Bernard Zeitler

In early 2013 I was in an accident. Hit broadside and tossed into the air followed by a head on collision with a tree. At the time it was believed that my wife and I should have, at the very least, needed an ambulance. Some felt we were 'lucky'. Interestingly what they believed was not what was actually true.

In the car we were injured but able to walk away with only injuries that were minor. As we were experiencing the accident we believed our lives were likely over, but again that was not the truth.

Often we think that because of 'x' that 'y' is true. This doesn't work in life. For example, when I started my recovery from Compulsive Gambling I believed I would never have a good life again. Yet here I am over 7 years later and life is getting better.

If you are going through something that you think you can't bear it, remember that it can get better. It will not be easy, but even if you repeat the mistake (relapse) it will get better.

Change Is Difficult But Often Necessary

Standing up for what's right is best when others are there with you."

Bernard Zeitler

Have you ever considered that changing habits are not always something done easily but often are necessary? When I first met my wife I was working the 'graveyard shift. It often turned into an even longer shift. This resulted in a significant change in sleeping habits. Having been diagnosed with asthma, this shift was even more difficult although it was also locked into my habits. Until a short time ago I was still 'off' when it came to sleep patterns.

My addiction was also like that. I had become accustom to the gambling and did not make the change easily. Even after being in the hospital due to the damage it caused I needed to get a 'wake up' call. My first meeting of GA was key. It was what I did immediately after that meeting that put me on the path to change. I left the meeting and gambled. At that point I crumbled. I realized that change was necessary. Do you have any experiences like that?

Just One Please!

If you could stop at just one, it would not change the problem only the frequency of it." Bernard Zeitler

For today's thought I'm returning to one of my old quotes.

Today **my wife** and I are going to the big city to take her brother out for a late lunch/ early dinner. Every time we go we see how skinny he his and think about how much he likes these visits.

We think he eats the best meals when he is with us so it has become a joy to visit with him. Have you ever felt that way?

When you go to your favorite place to eat a meal, can you order 'just one bite of food'? Do you find enjoyment in an entire meal? How about the experience?
Every time you go to this restaurant you find yourself entranced in the experience so going is not something you want to avoid. You might cut back to one time a week, month, year... but you don't stop entirely. So if the meal makes you sick the next day every time the result is the same. The only difference is how often you experience it.

This is what an addict experiences and why it is important to remember that even in recovery a relapse is possible. Going back once only changed the frequency not the problem.

What do you think?

Are You Waking Up?

"Addiction is like being in a coma. When you start recovery it is like you are waking up from the coma."

Bernard Zeitler

I know this is quote is from a while ago, but it was time to revisit it as a standalone.

Have you ever had a dream where you are waking up. Everything that is going on in the dream fits. Your normal habit, but it doesn't feel quite right. Then just as you think you are about to have something happen... you really wake up.

When you are in a n addiction it is like that dream. Everything seems right but you just aren't sure. Then you start recovery and you are 'really' awake. All those things that you used to do that were destroying your life are now 'taboo' for you.

Starting recovery is like coming out of a coma with the fear that you could slip back into it or that you are still in it and have been imagining it all. What change in life has been giving you a challenge to keep on that path?

Challenges Change Us

"Trials bring about new strength in previously unknown alliances."

Bernard Zeitler

Over the years I've lost friends, family, pets and more. It only seemed to open up opportunity to be affected by someone new. When we are going through a challenge it is hard to see past the problem, but if we look at the problem as part of a bigger opportunity it becomes much different.

I am Bernie and I am a recovering Compulsive Gambler. I've lost what I can't even remember but I've gained so much more. Each moment is more valuable than what was lost in the past and I cherish every moment because I can see clearly the mortality of it. Over time I have met people that are in my life who never would have been if not for that challenge.

Can you see something good in this moment that has to do with a past challenge in life?

Dogs, People And The Chase

"A dog chases their tail like people chase wealth."

Bernard Zeitler

You've seen it. A dog chasing their tail and just when they seem to catch it, it gets away! Much of life is that way. We 'chase' many different things and after our own desires with veracity. Just when we think we have everything we want, we find something new to chase after.

It is a human condition. I'm a recovering compulsive gambler and have watched as everything I needed was lost chasing after what I desired. In recovery my desires are simply focused on this moment and not on what I can get by 'chasing' something that is always just out of reach.

What do you chase after? Is it money, fame, gold, silver, food, or something your neighbor has? How do you remind yourself that this moment is all that matters?

Love And Pride

"Where love and pride meet life ends."

Bernard Zeitler

Have you ever needed help but did not allow yourself to ask for it? People who love each other tend to be less than willing to ask for help when they need it. In Gamblers Anonymous I learned that if I am too proud to reach out to those who love and care about me, it only destroys everything.

If I love someone I must be willing to put aside my pride when necessary. It is sometimes hard because Pride and Love are both ingrained in who we are.

What have you fought pride for that has hurt relationships? Have you ever been in love with your own pride?

Thought For Today: Losing While Gaining

"If you lose everything you have you have more than when you had everything."

Bernard Zeitler

Ok so some people might say how can losing everything and have more than you had before? A person who loses excess weight feel better and have more energy, so if that can be applied to other things wouldn't it have the same results?

I lost myself in gambling but in recovery I have gained so much more. When I was gambling I lost family, friends and self-respect just to name a few things. I started recovery as a broken man who could not seem to get anything right. At least that is what I thought.

Today I have a 'family' which spans the globe in the form of all my fellows who are also fighting their addiction. I have a wife who is supportive of me in ways that were missing in my previous marriage. My self-respect has been realigned to accept failure. The gains I have after being completely destroyed are beyond anything I could have ever imagined.

What losses have resulted in more gains for you?

Fear Of Change A Thought For Today

"What is scarier today? The pain you know or the challenge of getting to a better place."

Bernard Zeitler

Have you ever been so comfortable with what you are living that change scared you even though it was desired?

Often we get comfortable with a situation without realizing that is what is happening. For me it was an addiction. It became the norm and I was used to the pain that resulted from it. It made no difference how much pain I was experiencing as a result because it was what I 'knew'. When I realized things could be better I was eager to change but so scared that it was an unknown future.

People have a need for familiarity and when challenged by the thought of making a change it becomes scary. In recovery it is an unknown future that is the biggest deterrent to change. Focusing on the long term can scare us back to old habits. It has to become a desire to hold onto the moment in those early days because looking too far ahead is scary.

So back to the question are you afraid of Change?

An Accident Waiting To Happen?

"Addiction is a car accident waiting to happen. Recovery is the repair program."

Bernard Zeitler

In life we tend to have things that are so invasive that they 'control' our decision making process. It might be the time you spend getting prepared for the day, a routine of coffee drinking or almost anything. So the question is can we change that pattern?

Most people would say yes, some would say no. Here is the situation for an addict. They often find themselves at a point where they know that change must happen. For me I have spent my time since starting recovery focusing on how life change affects the routine. I am continually working at the 'repair program'.

What is changing in your life that you are looking at as part of that 'repair program'?

At This Moment!

"It matters not if you slipped in recovery, only that in this moment you are part of the recovery. In this moment I know people who have this moment clean."

Bernard Zeitler

Compulsive Gamblers have no reason to feel bad if they are clean at this moment. I am a compulsive gambler and I am NOT cured because at any time I could go back to gambling. I am in remission. I know that it seems hard for an addict to stay clean because it is always calling you I am confident in this moment that I am clean. I have decide to consider this thought:

I am one person in this moment and if there re 3,599 others also clean and in recovery at this moment I am part of a combined clean time of 1 hour (in this moment).

Be encouraged because I have confidence that there are 3, 599 othes who are recovering who are a part of the combined time so In this moment I am a part of at least one hour of clean time (again In this moment.)

It took me about 10 minutes to write this so in the time I wrote this with respect to combined time (If there are only 3,599 others) the total clean time is 25 Days!

Just Be In This Moment

"Recovery is awareness of this moment and not getting too far ahead of it."

Bernard Zeitler

I know it is normal to plan well into the future, but for some things it is best to just be in the moment you're in. As I started my recovery from Compulsive Gambling, I tried to look well into the future. My first meeting had me thinking I was not so bad. It only took me an instant to realize I was worse. I tried looking too far ahead and when I left that first meeting I gambled. It a split second I crumbled.

I became aware that I was not only like other Compulsive Gamblers I was unable to look beyond the moment. Is there anything in your life that you plan for and discover it was not what it seemed? How do you stay 'grounded' in this moment?

Imperfection Redeemed By Perfection

"The best bet is the one not made. Be, in this moment, the best you."

Bernard Zeitler

As a recovering Compulsive Gambler I know that I'm not perfect. All I can do is be the best 'me' in this moment. What I also know is that since I am imperfect I am not able to redeem myself. Good Friday is the day celebrated that the price has been paid. Jesus redeems us despite our flaws and before we have even accepted it.

What is your moment to appreciate? Do you accept the price is paid before you could even know the debt exists?

Never Again!!

"Saying 'Never Again' is really saying 'Maybe Tomorrow'. Since never will never come to pass!"

Bernard Zeitler

Often we make a mistake and say we will NEVER DO THAT AGAIN, but at some point in the future we do it again. Have you ever said 'never again' only do do that same thing at some point in the future?

An example is when you get pulled over for speeding or some other driving infraction. In the back of your head you might say I'm going to watch my speed better (or whatever the infraction is). Does it work? Over the years you are bound to repeat it. It isn't something you plan you just do it without considering what you said before. If you do remember, you may repeat the 'never again' vow. It is likely that it will be done again anyway. It may not happen again that day or week but you still repeat it.

What is your 'never again'? Can you change the thought to I'm not doing it again in this moment?

Another Thought For The Day

"The Biggest 'win' is when you 'lose'. 'Denial' forces a reality check daily."

Bernard Zeitler

Does it make sense that losing is winning? Some would say no, but I propose that it is the only sensible thing in life.

When we deny our desires in favor of our needs doesn't it end up being better? In America and other Developed nations sometimes we get wrapped up with keeping up with what someone else has. It often drives us to debt spending. In an effort to 'look' successful to others we accumulate what we do not need and lose some things that we truly need.

What do you think?

Day 4

Day 5:

Day 6:

Day 7:

Day 8:

Day 9:

Day 10:

Day 11:

Day 12:

Day 13:

Day 14:

Day 15:

Day 16:

Day 17:

Day 18:

Day 19:

Day 20:

Day 21:

Day 22:

Day 23:

Day 24:

Day 25:

Day 26:

Day 27:

Day 28:

Day 29:

Day 30:

After Detox:
The Next 90 Days

Addiction and Recovery In Five Short Chapters

1.

I head toward my addiction.
The addiction is a deep hole
I fall into it.
I am lost... I feel helpless.
I blame others.
It takes forever to escape it.

2.

I head toward the addiction again.
The addiction is still a deep hole.
I pretend it does not exist.
I fall into it again.
I can't believe I am back in the hole but, I still blame others.
It again takes forever to escape.

3.

I head toward the addiction again.
I see the deep hole of Addiction.
I pretend it is not there
I still fall in ...it is a patterned habit.
I see it clearly
I know this place.
I take responsibility for it. I escape immediately.

4.

I head toward the addiction again. I see the deep hole of
addiction I avoid it at the last second.

5.

I change my path avoiding the addiction entirely.

Introduction

After reading this introduction, read one thought each day for the next 90 days. The order of them is not important. Write down your impressions twice a day or more if you are so inclined.

In the life of a compulsive gambler is the story of stumbling and getting back up. If you have read 'The 30 Day Detox For Gamblers" or any of my previous books it becomes clear that hope is in the focus and energy we put into that recovery. In "After Detox, The Next 90 Days!" I expand on the idea of setting forth on that process. Here you will find 90 more of my sayings initially I will write on the quote. After 35 It's your turn.. The intention is to continue training your mind to create something personal and unique to you.

Without further ado here are 90 thoughts for the day to help you move into recovery. As you read them begin to think about what you would say to yourself to keep from gambling (or whatever your addiction is). Remember that making it personal is what will make it stick with you. It does not have to make any sense to anyone but you. The key is not in who said the thought but how it resonates with you. I am going to refer to this process as 'giving yourself advice". It is important to have support to stay clean in every form you can find. By doing your own thought for the day it's like calling yourself when the urge comes on. It can only help if you listen to it. If your mind is made up then no one can talk you out of it but they will be there when you come back. What I have found since starting recovery is that by starting the day with a personal thought, I talk myself out of the urge before it has a chance. It has been very helpful. If you did not catch it before my last bet was November 21, 2007 and using this process I have stayed away from relapse even as I worked at a job that required me to sell people lottery tickets for the first few years.

After Detox… The Next 90 Days!

Over Confidence

"If you can live without air then you can gamble without losing."
Bernard Zeitler

As a child there was a practice of holding your breath until you got what you wanted. The problem is that we lose consciousness if we hold it too long. It seldom if ever was successful. As adults we have some things we hold onto until it hurts without realizing that we are 'holding our breath' to get what we want.

If we go to an 'all you can eat restaurant' do we feel the need to eat more so we 'get our monies worth'? There are plenty of people who do indeed do that. The same thing happens with addiction.

As a compulsive gambler, I was intent on keeping the action going until I 'made my money back' or 'won big'. It was a false hope that took disaster to break. Remember the idea that we need to breathe more than we 'need' those things that prevent us from living a good life.

Living An Illusion

"Believing a lie doesn't make it true and denying the truth only hurts your own life." Bernard Zeitler

In life what we see is not always what is real. Have you ever heard or saw something that you believed without question only to find out it wasn't what it appeared?

In addiction this is common because it is the 'lie' that seems real for a time. In politics this 'illusion' is used to get votes. We are offered something for nothing often after the election it isn't there. In life if we believe something and think it is true only to find it to be a lie it hurts. How do you deal with the truth when t is not what you 'want' it to be?

Together We Can

"Just because I can't do it alone doesn't make me weak." Bernard Zeitler

Well I realized that my first 'Thought for Today" was a repeat of yesterday. It still applies but I try not to repeat the same thing 2 days in a row. When I come to an awareness of the thought I want to share it is often because of reading someone who shared their experiences.

The Thought for Today series I started because of a desire to have my mind on something that is encouraging and to share those thoughts with others who are struggling. I couldn't do it without others. But as the thought I am sharing says, I'm not weak because I need others to inspire me. It is precisely the fact that I need others that makes me strong. Remember: in weakness we are strong.

Recovery Is Not A One Time Thing

"Recovery is time sensitive, every moment matters." Bernard Zeitler

In life we realize that time is a fluid and changing. As a child we depend on others to care for us. As adults we learn to take care of ourselves and children (if we have them). But there is a time when we grow older and again depend on others. Depending on health issues that dependence may be different, but it is still there.

Can we accept that our life is a matter of living each moment as if it were the most important one we have? Can we see that every moment is a process of recovering from the moment that came before it? How are you 'living in this moment'?

Toilet Paper And Life

"Life is like a roll of toilet paper. You are constantly rolling along with the potential to be flushed." Bernard Zeitler

Have you ever thought about how Life is constantly changing? Life continually 'rolls' out new experiences and it we are not prepared we can have troubles that will 'flush' our hopes.

Last night I was feeling a bit down and realized that change, even when you want it has an effect on your perspective. It is often very difficult to realize that as life 'rolls' along the past is gone and our future is still hidden in the 'roll'. All we have is now and yet we need to prepare for the future enough to know we are not at a loss. How are you at letting life roll out before you and letting the past go so that you are ready for the present.. What is your thoughts on life and the comparison of Toilet Paper?

It's Not About How Long

"Be proud of this moment clean, not in the amount of time clean. This moment is the one that matters most right now." Bernard Zeitler

I am a Compulsive Gambler in Recovery. An addict who is 'clean' right now. so which is more important? That I have been 'clean' since November 21, 2007 or that I am clean right now?

There is a riddle about which came first... The Chicken or the egg. Does it really matter today? We have both and can enjoy the chicken as a meal and the egg as a meal. People eat both but does it matter to you when you are hungry which came first?

In my recovery I know when my last bet was but it does not change that I gambled in the past or that I am not gambling now. What matters to me and to those who love me is that I am not gambling right now. I've heard people get upset about a relapse after having been 'clean' for days, weeks, months and years. I can't change that, but I can change right now. Right now I have decided in this moment to be 'clean' I can't worry about what might happen or what has already happened. So here is my key to having been clean for years: It only matters that I am not gambling right now. When the anniversaries come I will celebrate them but I will remain focused on right now because it is all that I can control.

How about you? Are there things you have milestones that you celebrate that you focus on without thinking about the moment you are in?

Never Again!

"Saying 'Never Again' is really saying 'Maybe Tomorrow'. Since never will never come to pass!" Bernard Zeitler

Often we make a mistake and say we will NEVER DO THAT AGAIN, but at some point in the future we do it again. Have you ever said 'never again' only do do that same thing at some point in the future?

An example is when you get pulled over for speeding or some other driving infraction. In the back of your head you might say I'm going to watch my speed better (or whatever the infraction is). Does it work? Over the years you are bound to repeat it. It isn't something you plan you just do it without considering what you said before. If you do remember, you may repeat the 'never again' vow. It is likely that it will be done again anyway. It may not happen again that day or week but you still repeat it.

What is your 'never again'? Can you change the thought to I'm not doing it again in this moment?

Temptation And Time In Recovery

"Discouragement is temporary, recovery is in the moment and long term."
Bernard Zeitler

Often in a moment of distress a person gravitates toward their addiction. In that moment it is important to focus on why we are in recovery. Doing that often will help hold the moment and make it through even if only 'by the skin of our teeth'. In so doing we survive for the long term as opposed to fall into the temporary solution that only makes things worse.

What is that fallback position for you when you become discouraged? Is it: Chocolate Pop/ Soda Food Gambling Dispute Sleep

How do you remember the moment?

Patience In The Moment

"Patience is Recovery in the moment of an urge. It is better to put a penny in the slot of a piggy bank than a machine in that moment."
Bernard Zeitler

Have you ever had an urge to eat a piece of chocolate or any favorite food?
How about to do a favorite activity?
I have heard and seen over time how my compulsive gambling and other activities have driven me when I allow the 'urge' control the 'moment'. It seldom ends up being as good as I thought it would be. When it did, it did not last. Some days there is an urge to get things done faster than they should be done, but I've learned to allow myself to be in the moment rather than in the urge. What challenges do you experience when the urge collides with the moment you are in?

Just Be In This Moment

"Recovery is awareness of this moment and not getting too far ahead of it."
Bernard Zeitler

I know it is normal to plan well into the future, but for some things it is best to just be in the moment you're in. As I started my recovery from Compulsive Gambling, I tried to look well into the future. My first meeting had me thinking I was not so bad. It only took me an instant to realize I was worse. I tried looking too far ahead and when I left that first meeting I gambled. It a split second I crumbled.
I became aware that I was not only like other Compulsive Gamblers I was unable to look beyond the moment. Is there anything in your life that you plan for and discover it was not what it seemed? How do you stay 'grounded' in this moment?

Words And Actions

"Your words may say one thing but are your actions in agreement?"
Bernard Zeitler

Often we hear people making promises, telling what they believe
and discussing their day. The question came to me: Is it
synchronized? Do the words and actions fit? Jesus addressed this
regularly.

He overturned tables in the synagogue when money changers and
salesmen were corrupting it. 2, A group of men brought an adulteress
to him for stoning and he reminded them of their sins.

The disciples said things and were reminded of what it meant.

When we get so confident that we say something without acting in a
way that is consistent with it our words fall silent. I try to remember
what my actions should be when I say something, but sometimes I
forget that connection. How are you doing with this?

Imperfection Redeemed By Perfection

"The best bet is the one not made. Be, in this moment, the best you."
Bernard Zeitler

As a recovering Compulsive Gambler I know that I'm not perfect. All I can do is be the best 'me' in this moment. What I also know is that since I am imperfect I am not able to redeem myself. Good Friday is the day celebrated that the price has been paid. Jesus redeems us despite our flaws and before we have even accepted it.

What is your moment to appreciate? Do you accept the price is paid before you could even know the debt exists?

Change Is Difficult But Often Necessary

"Standing up for what's right is best when others are there with you."
Bernard Zeitler

Have you ever considered that changing habits are not always something done easily but often are necessary? When I first met my wife in 2012, I was working the 'graveyard shift. It often turned into an even longer shift. This resulted in a significant change in sleeping habits. Having been diagnosed with asthma, this shift was even more difficult although it was also locked into my habits. Until a short time ago I was still 'off' when it came to sleep patterns.

My addiction was also like that. I had become accustom to the gambling and did not make the change easily. Even after being in the hospital due to the damage it caused I needed to get a 'wake up' call. My first meeting of GA was key. It was what I did immediately after that meeting that put me on the path to change. I left the meeting and gambled. At that point I crumbled. I realized that change was necessary. Do you have any experiences like that?

Dogs, People And The Chase

"A dog chases their tail like people chase wealth." Bernard Zeitler

You've seen it. A dog chasing their tail and just when they seem to catch it, it gets away! Much of life is that way. We 'chase' many different things and after our own desires with veracity. Just when we think we have everything we want, we find something new to chase after.
It is a human condition. I'm a recovering compulsive gambler and have watched as everything I needed was lost chasing after what I desired. In recovery my desires are simply focused on this moment and not on what I can get by 'chasing' something that is always just out of reach.
What do you chase after? Is it money, fame, gold, silver, food, or something your neighbor has? How do you remind yourself that this moment is all that matters?

Losing While Gaining

"If you lose everything you have you have more than when you had everything." Bernard Zeitler

Ok so some people might say how can losing everything and have more than you had before? A person who loses excess weight feel better and have more energy, so if that can be applied to other things wouldn't it have the same results?

I lost myself in gambling but in recovery I have gained so much more. When I was gambling I lost family, friends and self-respect just to name a few things. I started recovery as a broken man who could not seem to get anything right. At least that is what I thought.

Today I have a 'family' which spans the globe in the form of all my fellows who are also fighting their addiction. I have a wife who is supportive of me in ways that were missing in my previous marriage. My self-respect has been realigned to accept failure. The gains I have after being completely destroyed are beyond anything I could have ever imagined.

What losses have resulted in more gains for you?

A Hidden Treasure Found

"If addiction has a loss of personal value Then Recovery is the Rebirth of value hidden." Bernard Zeitler

As I remember those days when I was 'in' my addiction, I recall losing who I was. I let feelings determine my value. It was a downhill trip because as each day passed I found more things to hide from and more ways to cut myself down. I thought I was ok but forgot that I was not ok.
In recovery I was 'reborn'. I found that focusing on this moment allowed me to see what was right in front of me. I can see that there is more challenge and enjoyment in life when I am not gambling.

What hidden treasure have you found by getting past a habit that keeps you from seeing it?

Tools

"Any tool is only as effective as the person using it. A tool must also be customized by the user." Bernard Zeitler

When a person is trying to change or break a habit it is important to build a 'tool box'. We can use things others have done, but unless we adapt the tool it is not going to 'fit'.

I have begun a formalized project to test that principal. After writing "The 30 Day Detox For Gamblers". My belief is that along with other therapeutic processes, changing perspective is necessary.

The book shares how I did that and makes it more formal. The key to the process involves the individual finding their own thought for today which reminds them of their goal. In the first 30 days it is hard to do that and so the book walks them through those days and encourages the reader to make the 'tool' personal. It then becomes a customized version which improves the success of the tool.

What do you think?

Love And Pride

"Where love and pride meet life ends." Bernard Zeitler

Have you ever needed help but did not allow yourself to ask for it? People who love each other tend to be less than willing to ask for help when they need it. In Gamblers Anonymous I learned that if I am too proud to reach out to those who love and care about me, it only destroys everything. If I love someone I must be willing to put aside my pride when necessary. It is sometimes hard because Pride and Love are both ingrained in who we are.

What have you fought pride for that has hurt relationships? Have you ever been in love with your own pride?

Fear Of Change

What is scarier today? The pain you know or the challenge of getting to a better place." Bernard Zeitler

Have you ever been so comfortable with what you are living that change scared you even though it was desired?

Often we get comfortable with a situation without realizing that is what is happening. For me it was an addiction. It became the norm and I was used to the pain that resulted from it. It made no difference how much pain I was experiencing as a result because it was what I 'knew'. When I realized things could be better I was eager to change but so scared that it was an unknown future.

People have a need for familiarity and when challenged by the thought of making a change it becomes scary. In recovery it is an unknown future that is the biggest deterrent to change. Focusing on the long term can scare us back to old habits. It has to become a desire to hold onto the moment in those early days because looking too far ahead is scary.

So back to the question: Are you afraid of Change?

The Importance Of Being Present!

"Make now your priority and you will survive it." Bernard Zeitler

I remember a time when I was looking so far ahead that I missed the hole in front of me. I remember a time when I was always looking behind me and I ran into a wall in front of me.
I have made it a point to do what I need to right now, realizing I made mistakes in my past and knowing that tomorrow is dependent on today. While I plan ahead, it is with a focus on this moment. If I get too far ahead of myself I lose focus on where I am. If I look back too much I can't function because my mistakes can overwhelm me.

What are you doing to be in the present?

Underwear Recovery

"Recovery is like underwear, you might have the same brand as someone else but it doesn't fit the same." Bernard Zeitler

I know underwear seems a bit odd to describe Recovery, but think about it for a moment.

I am a compulsive gambler, but I am not the only one. Some compulsive gamblers are Casino focused others (like me) are scratch off tickets. The addiction is the same but the path to get there is different. In recovery we are all looking for the same results but our experience in getting there is bound to have differences. We can use the same tools, but differently. The tools are best when we customize them to our journey. For me I review the 12 steps daily but not always in the same order. I might wake up feeling guilty about who has been hurt so Amends are my starting point. I focus on where I am in that moment and move forward from there.

My recovery starts each morning with a thought for recovery. It changes me throughout the day.

What is your starting point today?

Rolling In The Mud

"I'm 'clean' right now and I don't want to roll in mud so I'll stay focused"
Bernard Zeitler

Sometimes I start to think about the stuff I did to 'hide' from the important parts of my life. Family, friends, and life in general. The problems is I also had to hide the muddied messes I caused. Today I have kept myself away from Gambling. I still struggle, but not in the same way.
I focus on facing things in my life and not making a mess while hiding from what I thought was the real mess. So I remember each moment of recovery as if it is that first breath of fresh air after a cleansing rain. I see life as a rainbow of promise ahead as long as I focus on this moment.

So are you focusing on right now or are you in the mud to hide from it?

Can You See The Cost?

"Recovery is not free or easy, but addiction is expensive and Difficult"
Bernard Zeitler

First, I would like to say that while money is behind the addiction, it is not the greatest cost. I am about to share some of the story of my recovery. I worked at a convenience store for several years and almost lost my job because of my addiction. I kept my job thanks to a caring and aware manager, but not before I ended up in adult psych for Suicidal Depression. After 10 days in the unit, I went to 2 more weeks of outpatient treatment. During this time I lost family and associates. My ex-wife found out just how bad my gambling was and a business I was launching failed.

I returned to my job but at a different location and continued for several years to sell the very thing that caused my destruction.

Today I am married to a wonderful wife who has gone through some difficulties with me. My health has deteriorated to the point that I am unable to work and that puts a lot of stress on her.

Much of my life has been rebuilt, but some things are gone for good. My mother died before I started recovery and I missed spending time with her in those last days. My father and I were able to repair some of the damage and I was holding his hand when he died.

So remember what your addiction has cost you and consider what recovery will cost and how much better it will be.

Alone In A Crowd

"If you died winning would it be worth being alone?" Bernard Zeitler

Consider this. If you have an addiction and you are all alone in a crowd is it healthy? When I was gambling I shut out all my problems for that time but they were always waiting for me after I was done. Sometimes they were worse.

While many people were around me, I was only aware of myself in those moments. I could not get past it. So in recovery I am never alone even in an 'empty' room. I think of others who are fighting their addictions. I know where people who care are and they know where I am. I may have lost people because of my addiction, but consequences are not going to change and it does not get better overnight. All I can say is winning is no longer about the action of gambling. I will not be alone in my journey and can accept that I will not always have people physically with me. What are your thoughts on this?

If You Always Win...

"If you have won more than you've lost then you're the house because it always wins." Bernard Zeitler

I just finished reading a friend's writing. It is a sign that "The 30 Day Detox For Gamblers" works well. It is intended to teach self-awareness and development of thoughts upon waking up. Some have shown this tendency and it is a great influence on recovery..

What Dawn wrote spoke to the idea of crossing the line blindly. So often people think of gambling addiction as involving money. Her writing speaks to the mind triggering an excitement that is not readily aware when you are gambling. In 'How To Win As A High Roller While Losing Your Shirt" I point out that the addiction to gambling was there as a child playing marbles on the playground. It is important to know that Gambling Addiction is not about money.

About a week ago I began a journey of testing the formalization of the practice. With a group of fellow Compulsive Gamblers who have experienced repeated failure. Those who are embracing it are doing well as far as I can tell.

I don't know if Dawn was aware of what I was trying to instill in her several months ago, but it appears she is internalizing it. Her "Thought For Today" really affected me. I know the things she was talking about but to hear that someone else has seen it is encouraging.

Here is the point I am making with the above quote. As a Compulsive Gambler we reported our wins but seldom if ever reported our losses. This was our 'House' of Imaginary success. The reality was that people who have control of our addictions don't lose. The Casino, State, Bookie etc. always 'Wins".

In recovery each moment not gambling is a win so at that point we again become the 'House' but now it is about our sanity and wellbeing. Staying clean is always a win and it is the best win of our lives because it is not imaginary but real!

So are you The 'House' with your recovery?

Addiction By Proxy?

"Proxy Gambling is still Gambling! Have you been vicariously Gambling?"
Bernard Zeitler

I have heard people sys things like: I don't gamble anymore. I have
gone with a friend and watched them while they used my 'Perks' Card.
…. Wanted me to place a bet for them so I did, but I didn't gamble. I
don't go to the casino, I play the lottery/ raffle/ such and such game. I
am not gambling. All of these are Proxy Gambling. Even if no money is
involved in a 'game of chance' or other activity it can still be Gambling.
If you are purposefully assisting someone else to gamble in these ways
you may be gambling by proxy. Gambling is gambling whether it's with
your money, someone else's money or no money at all. Compulsive
gambling is not about the money in reality. It is about the action. I
worked in a convinced store when my world came apart. My form of
Gambling was Lottery tickets, scratch off to be exact. But for a boss
who liked me I would have lost my job. As things fell apart at work,
which is also where I gambled, Depression set in. I kept my job but
went into treatment for ten days. When I returned I was in a different
store. They knew of my addiction and I sold lottery tickets to
customers for until early in 2011 as a part of my job.
That is how I learned to work through it. I had to sell them. My fellow
employees and new boss knew of my difficulties. Most of the time they
intercepted the lottery sales, but when they didn't I found that I would
say to customers who I knew had a problem "The next one's a
winner!" Since customers knew my background it had an effect on
their gambling practices. Over time I became aware of a practice that I
shared with others informally when they asked how I could stay clean
while selling them. It resulted in my first book which set up the
foundation for the second book and a formalized process to help other
compulsive gamblers maintain sobriety. Informally it had over 90%
effectiveness. Now formalized and one week into the process it is
showing even better results.

So now is the question are you gambling by Proxy?

Selfie Recovery

"Repeat yourself when you are at your best, let go of yourself when you're not." Bernard Zeitler

In recovery we find ourselves reflecting on how we got where we are. The picture above is one of many I took to remember the house my father had built in his old age. It was a monument to his determination. He built it with minimal help in his 70's. It was his design, personal hands on crafting and labor. When he was young he built many homes. Each time people wanted to buy the one he was in thinking that it was better than the one he was selling because he had his family living in it. Each time he moved his family and let the person buy the one he was in.

Often this is how we live our lives, believing that someone does their best work for themselves. In recovery we need to be willing to let go of the idea that we have to hold onto our past mistakes as a part of our best successes. Let go of the things that you are beating yourself up over and embrace those things that are the best about you.

Keep doing what helps you get through the moment you are in. Share those successes with others and build upon them. This is why I share my personal story, thought for the day and anything else that will help others. It is the best of me.

Columbo Recovery

Columbo has a saying that he has said over and over in the series. He says "Whenever I get a hunch and ignore it, I regret it." I have an adaptation for Recovry: "Whenever I get a hunch or urge and I follow it, I regret it!" Bernard Zeitler with credit to Columbo...

Have you thought about that? As a Recovering Compulsive Gambler I have had 'hunches' and urges but I know that following them is something I ALWAYS regret. If I win I keep going and if I lose I keep going. It becomes a painful cycle. How do I stop? I stop by changing my mindset/ thought process. It is not something that happens overnight and it is not easy.

Often I think I already understand that but then I realize that my addiction is calling by changing my thought to the 'hunch' and the urge. So I encourage people to remember... When this happens if I follow, I regret!

Recovery Vs. Addiction

"Pick your poison carefully it could kill what is important to you." Bernard Zeitler

When I was in my addiction I was not so careful about who was affected. I was ready to follow it wherever it led me. As I started to recover, I realized what damage I had caused to myself and others. The poison of my addiction had killed relationships, jobs and people who saw me when I was gambling. The poison had not yet destroyed me but I had considered suicide.

As I went through the process of recovery I poisoned the addiction. It is now on 'life support' as it relates to me. I get the urges and thoughts but because of recovery it is not fed.

It took time but many relationships I thought were dead were revived. Now I have a far different view of the addiction. I have chosen to work to 'poison' it and not the good things in my life.

Bathroom Bets!

Gambling is like going to the bathroom. You will be lighter when you're done." Bernard Zeitler

How many times when I was in my addiction did I really have money when I was done? Did my Gambling really do anything for me other than make me feel like crap when I was done?
Gambling is not fun when you're done. At least when I come out of the bathroom I feel better (most of the time). After gambling, drinking or any addiction has taken its course it is not a relief, it's an anxiety fest! It's fun while it lasts but afterwards it really is crappy. That is the opposite of going to the bathroom. When you are done with that you leave the crap behind!

So what do you think?

Proud To Be Known For My Failure!

"I'm known for my failure…. To gamble!" Bernard Zeitler

The title is not one most people would write. Today, after over 7 years clean, I know I could go back but why. I have become known for not gambling anymore. People know that I am a recovering Compulsive Gambler because I make no secret of it.
I decided to fight for my sobriety by studying the addiction. This resulted in a number of things that I am very glad I did.
I began speaking thanks to the encouragement of Lori Mello a few years back.
I wrote my first book to help people understand the addiction in a way that makes it real to them. (How To Win As A High Roller While Losing Your Shirt)
I continue to write about this addiction.
After sharing a technique I use to stay clean (in a covert way) informally for several years, I have now written it out formally and published it (The 30
Day Detox For Gamblers)
I am preparing to write more books on the topic and focus on keeping the price as low as possible to make them accessible.
These are just a few of the things that have come from my decision to be known for my failure…. to Gamble. So as the title says, I'm proud to be known for my Failure.

Will you be proud to be known for your failure to continue in your addiction?

Lights Out Recovery!

"Recovery is like leaving a room at night, you need to remember to turn off the light." Bernard Zeitler

Today I was reminded of how easily a person can return to old habits. When the power went out, I went from room to room to do different projects. Even though the poser was out I still turned on the light switch. This made it harder to remember to turn them off as nothing happened in the first place.

When we are recovering from an addiction or any situation for that matter, do we remember to move forward and turn out the light? If we truly want to go forward can we turn off the light from the past so it doesn't give us a reason to go back?

The Importance Of Getting Back Up!

"A child's first steps are often wobbly and they fall down. Take their lead. Get back up after a slip." Bernard Zeitler

I did a study informally to see if this process would work and on day 14 of that study I wrote this thought for the people in the study. Consider the importance of getting back up after a slip as you read this. Can you share encouragement to someone who is struggling because you have experienced this?

When I did the informal trial it was at this point that most slips happened. Even so it was important to remember that we are just beginning. Our triggers still haunt us in the background, past failures haunt us and almost anything can set us back. Those who take heed of a child's example when taking those first steps can still be successful. Do not give up or forget that when things are fresh in the mind it can bring back hidden 'calls'

My youngest son had just begun walking when he fell off a swing and broke his leg setting back his running. Six weeks later the cast came off and he returned to practicing his walking. Having stuck with it he began walking quickly and learned from the experience... It is necessary when we fall down to get back up and use it as a lesson to make us stronger.

The Eyes Of The Beholder!

"Being blind is not always about seeing with your eyes." Bernard
Zeitler

I'd like to ask a question. Have you ever had your eyes wide open and
been able to see everything but still been blind? I have.

An example of what I'm talking about is all around us. I can see that
there is air but I really can't see it. An odor can be smelled but not seen.
Sound can be heard but not seen. Yet a few years ago I had a very
serious Sinus

infection. Because of my long history of Bronchitis and all the tests
indicated that is what I had, my regular Dr. diagnosed Bronchitis and
could not hear what I was saying as something else. A week later I was
back

because it was not getting better. I had a different Dr. who diagnosed
a

possible Sinus infection. The proper tests were ordered and the Dr.
was right. The difference.... She was blind. As a result her other senses
were used. She could 'see' what I was saying.

This is what it is for recovery, we need to always be alert. Look for what
is not seen and see what is not visible. It helps to be aware of
everything

going on because it can save you in a time when your thoughts and
urges are knocking on the 'door' of your old habits.

Now It Is Your Turn.

In my previous books I have explained how we have to make things personal. In the 30 Day Detox for Gamblers I shared 30 little articles just as the ones on previous pages. Here I have shared 35 more which leaves 55 days to the end of the 90n days covered here. If you did the 30 Day Detox this would bring you to 65 days clean.

In the next 56 pages (I added a Bonus quote) I will put a quote at the top of the page. It is up to you to write an interpretation of them. When you are done you should have about 120 days clean. If you slip, remember to get back up and restart the process. It is hoped that when you are done with this book you will keep going and find your own 'quotes', and thoughts to continue your recovery.

If at any time you want to let me know how you are doing or desire to ask a question there is information on how to reach me. I will respond as quickly as I can. When I am no longer able to do so I am hopeful someone will continue to answer the questions.

So here is your beginning! Turn the page and begin!

To 'bark' up the wrong tree is better than cutting down the right one.

To be broke at home is better than having money to lose in public.

Recovery in the beginning is scratching the surface of a missing past.

Recovery is new every day.

Change of opinion is necessary when the opinion involves going and gambling.

It is hard to sleep when an addiction is on your mind.

Recovery is best when: The addiction is not on your mind at bedtime or when you wake.

The difference between letting go and holding on is open arms.

Recovery is not about cash flow but about air flow.

Recovery is all in the landing.

A moment in recovery may not be pleasant but you are still on the journey.

Each moment is a new moment of growth.

What I do is not always who I am.

When faced with change, pocket it before you lose it.

If you come to a familiar fork in the road, remember not to repeat the painful one.

Before you do something familiar, remember to breathe.

Why play when it will spark a blaze that is hard to put out.

A lonely day is not when you're alone but when you're in a crowd and don't care.

Encourage yourself by remembering yourself.

Be an antidote when a cure is not visible.

If it hurts now imagine how bad it was when you were hiding.

If you think recovery is hard try relapse it's harder.

Not all who gamble are addicts, but all addicts are gamblers.

Addiction is not a weakness, it's a disease of the mind and body.

A consequence of recovery is living with a real world view.

Even the right path has a few bumps in it.

There are battles that are small moral victories to provide a better chance to win the war.

When fighting for right, choose your gear carefully and consider the future.

Recovery is like finding a hidden treasure, it's more valuable than anything in the world.

When you find what you're looking for it's never too late.

To lose everything is to gain everything that's real.

If you're still alive when you reach out for help it isn't too late.

You don't have to know someone to help them, but if you don't know yourself it's harder.

When this moment is in doubt, remember you're not alone.

A mind is not wasted unless it is not used.

Addiction, disease and infection all have two things in common. They can all be treated and they can all kill.

Remembering is fluid when you are deciding on an action. But repeat mistakes tend to hurt like a solid memory.

Focus is key when trying to avoid repeating the past.

Being tempted is human, fighting temptation is divine help.

The only path to recovery is through the valley of bottoming out.

Every person finds their own last time that leads to recovery.

Memorial Day can be the day of new beginnings.

Recovery is work, but when the load is shared it gets easier.

**If you learn something that helps share it in your own personal.
Making change personal makes it more likely to be successful.**

Just as a person can get over confident in recovery, so it is with meetings.

Consider the difference between what is real and what is imagined.

Time outs are for pets, children and addicts in recovery.

Recovery may have bumps in the road, but addiction is a deep hole that takes a lot of help to escape.

A slip happens but it takes effort to fall.

To protect yourself you must first know what the problem is.

To know the truth you need to recognize a lie first.

In recovery as in business it is not wise to say something without being sure of it.

Recovery requires an intense desire to focus on this moment clean!

A colon can indicate a pause, painful stoppage or the runs. It's all in your perspective.

When you run out of strength it is important to remember you are not alone.

Today is lived one breath at a time. Yesterday has already been exhaled. Don't try to revive it.

Everything you did to gamble just shows what you can do for recovery.

At this moment you are not alone even if no one is with you.

Bernard Zeitler

THE LIFE RECOVERY JOURNAL

Introduction

Recovery from any situation is hard, but as a recovering compulsive gambler I find myself working daily to keep finding new ways to focus on the day and moment at hand. That is why I began writing.

At some point I realized that we all have a journey that we take and any tool we can get is a good thing.

In 2013 I finally started getting my life back on track with a new Bride and a revived desire to help understand the life of addiction and recovery. As a result I finished my first book and soon found myself wanting to do more.

As my research, soul searching and focus was developing after November 21 2007, I found that people could relate to what I wrote. I stopped caring about being 'perfect' in the written word. It began as a personal journey to regain my faith, integrity and educational background. Today I have found something greater. I have found fellowship with people around the world.

As a result of that my books have helped me see what I was hiding from in my addiction. This book is built on the principles and work of those that came before.

"How To Win As A High Roller While Losing Your Shirt" started as an attempt to tell my story and became a workbook to help give people (addict or not) an understanding of what is happening.

After some struggling with what next, I came to the conclusion that I needed to develop tools for the addict to use when they were ready. This gave birth to the next three books which shared a system

I used to get back my sanity.

First came "The 30 Day Detox For Gamblers" which shared

the technique.

Then ""The Path To Recovery Program" which further defined the process and combined both of my previous books into one product for recovery.

Once that was done it became clear that recovery takes time to become strong. I remembered that I was still very weak after that first 30 days and needed to get to 120 days. That gave birth to the next project.

"After Detox: The next 90 Days became a program to give people time to learn the practice of having a personal thought each morning to keep them going.

Now we are at this book. Often books are written to give a person something to read each day to keep going. In light of that this book is intended to give thoughts to think about each day to keep focused. It is a journal because while there is a thought shared, the reader picks the one the will use each day and write their own thoughts on what it means to them. It becomes their own focus not that of someone else.

So here is the overview:

This book has one of the thoughts I use to get through the day. They are all my own personal thoughts but unlike in the previous books I have not written anything about the thought. That is your job. You can reuse any of them as many times as you want. I suggest writing what the words mean to you at 3 different times during the day. Every so often use the poem that follows to remind yourself of where you are in your recovery.

I suggest one thing above all else....Don't Let your guard down and think you have beaten this! If you slip get back on track. Make note of what happened and don't beat yourself up for it. Realize that you must have let your guard down.

Addiction and Recovery In Five Short Chapters

1.

I head toward my addiction.
The addiction is a deep hole
I fall into it.
I am lost... I feel helpless.
I blame others.
It takes forever to escape it.

2.

I head toward the addiction again.
The addiction is still a deep hole.
I pretend it does not exist.
I fall into it again.
I can't believe I am back in the hole
but, I still blame others.
It again takes forever to escape.

3.

I head toward the addiction again.
I see the deep hole of Addiction.
I pretend it is not there
I still fall in ...it is a patterned habit.
I see it clearly
I know this place.
I take responsibility for it.
I escape immediately.

4.

I head toward the addiction
again. I see the deep hole of
addiction I avoid it at the last
second.

5.

I change my path avoiding the addiction entirely.

I woke up this morning and in this moment I am one of thousands of people who are not gambling in this moment. As a result the combined time is one day. I am part of a day clean in each moment I am clean.

The pot of gold at the end of the rainbow is as much an illusion as the high of Addiction. The best high in life is the breath you take in this moment and it will never make a promise it can't keep either?

When you are sitting in the corner of your room contemplating your addiction it is easier to see the lie than to recognize the truth. Until you recognize the truth your contemplation is over and recovery begins.

If addiction has a loss of personal value Then Recovery is the Rebirth of value hidden.

When an addict believes they are 'cured', they are ripe for 'relapse'. Recovery isn't just about the time but also about the awareness.

There is hope for recovery in each breath you take. Relapse only means you need to get back to treating your addiction.

Saying 'Never Again' is rally saying 'Maybe Tomorrow'. Since never will never come to pass!

The Biggest 'win' is when you 'lose'. 'Denial' forces a reality check daily.

Winning is as rare as Admitting loss. Every "System" has a flaw that you ignore.

Addiction is a car accident waiting to happen. Recovery is the repair program.

Sleeping Addictions can only wake up with an untreated urge.

The best bet is the one not made. Be, in this moment, the best you.

Recovery is awareness of this moment and not getting too far ahead of it.

Rolling away the obstructions to recovery takes persistence.

An old story is only as valuable as the lesson you learn from it.

Patience is Recovery in the moment of an urge. It is better to put a penny in the slot of a piggy bank than a machine in that moment.

When you've lost everything you didn't know you had recovery finds you.

Discouragement is temporary, recovery is in the moment and long term.

Life is like a roll of toilet paper. You are constantly rolling along with the potential to be flushed.

Recovery is time sensitive, every moment matters.

Be proud of this moment clean, not in the amount of time clean. This moment is the one that matters most right now.

If you can live without air then you can gamble without losing.

Believing a lie doesn't make it true and denying the truth only hurts your own life.

Just because I can't do it alone doesn't make me weak.

Your words may say one thing but are your actions in agreement?

What we think is true doesn't make it true.

If you could stop at just one, it would not change the problem only the frequency of it.

Addiction is like being in a coma. When you start recovery it is like you are waking up from the coma.

Standing up for what's right is best when others are there with you.

Trials bring about new strength in previously unknown alliances.

A dog chases their tail like people chase wealth.

Where love and pride meet life ends.

If you lose everything you have you have more than when you had everything.

What is scarier today? The pain you know or the challenge of getting to a better place.

When I run I have to consider if it is in the right direction.

Life is all about learning how to be who you really are.

Losing is more fun than winning in recovery. Losing the addiction to the moment of recovery has great value!

Knowing your weakness doesn't prevent it from interrupting recovery. Accepting it helps more.

Miracles happen, just not the Way we call them.

Disappointment happens but it doesn't have to define you.

Addiction is like a hot cookie if you are not careful you'll get burned.

The path we walk depends upon the balance we have.

Wanting something good doesn't mean it's good for you.

Being aware of yourself is important in life.

Any tool is only as effective as the person using it. A tool must also be customized by the user.

Now I am clean, that is all that matters.

Make now your priority and you will survive it.

Returning to the past sets you up to fail in the present moment.

Each day is a new beginning. It is important to be aware of that.

If you want to be 100% right you should first admit you are 100% wrong.

Recovery is like underwear. You might have the same brand as someone else but it doesn't fit the same.

Recovery is personal. It is like DNA once you have it you keep it for life.

Order and structure is good until it doesn't fit together.

Success is between disaster and hope.

Recovery is the journey for all of your life.

Today I am part of a family of recovery. Even failure is accepted. I just need to come back!

I'm 'clean' right now and I don't want to roll in mud so I'll stay focused.

Recovery is not free or Easy, but addiction is expensive and difficult.

It's Important to be with others in recovery, but not to the exclusion of those you missed while in your addiction.

To help a person in recovery one must consider the cost of their addiction.

To work diligently for the benefit of others is Nobel. Many may not care.

What is recovery if you can get a proxy rush?

If you died winning would it be worth being alone?

To gamble you must be willing to lose what matters more than money.

If you have won more than you've lost then you're the house because it always wins.

The only time you hear how much a person lost is:

When they are facing prison. Being beaten down by a bookie Or When they attempt suicide.

Life has challenges and troubles. Never avoid these opportunities to grow!

Addiction may be exciting but recovery is more exciting!

Proxy Gambling is still Gambling! Have you been vicariously Gambling?

Repeat yourself when you are at your best, let go of yourself when you're not.

One slip can lead to a painful fall.

This is recovery at its best, when you are supportive of a fellow traveler even as you're struggling.

Insanity is one trip away but recovery is in your hands.

Hope is when recovery begins to be possible.

Be willing to internalize thoughts of recovery. Then share your thought to encourage others.

Whenever I get a hunch or urge to gamble, If I follow it I regret it.!
(A play on something Columbo says often).

Pick your poison carefully it could kill what is important to you.

The cost of recovery is the nightmare for those selling the addiction to you.

I'm known for my failure…. To gamble!

A 'Free' perk is like a free Audit. They both are too expensive!

Gambling is like going to the bathroom. You will be lighter when you're done.

Gambling and garbage disposals are the same. They will take everything you give them.

Recovery is like leaving a room at night, you need to remember to turn off the light.

A child's first steps are often wobbly and they fall down. Take their lead. Get back up after a slip.

Recovery is like breathing exercises for Asthma. Without it you can die.

Your recovery is personal. Your addiction is painful... for everyone!

Know yourself in recovery and you will know the pain of your addiction.

Recovery is personal but community is key to individual success!

I desire recovery even when I need help standing alone.

When the fantasy of addiction ends the real recovery begins.

Unity is sharing your story with another person and listening to theirs.

Seeing is believing but believing is not seeing.

Being blind is not always about seeing with your eyes.

To 'bark' up the wrong tree is better than cutting down the right one.

To be broke at home is better than having money to lose in public.

Recovery in the beginning is scratching the surface of a missing past.

Recovery is new every day.

Coming out of addiction is the birth of a new life. A child of recovery at any age is still a child.

Change of opinion is necessary when the opinion involves going and gambling.

It is hard to sleep when an addiction is on your mind.

Recovery is best when: The addiction is not on your mind at bedtime or when you wake.

In recovery nervousness still haunts us at times because we were used to it before starting recovery.

The difference between letting go and holding on is open arms.

Recovery is not about cash flow but about air flow.

Recovery is all in the landing.

A moment in recovery may not be pleasant but you are still on the journey.

Each moment is a new moment of growth.

What I do is not always who I am.

When faced with change, pocket it before you lose it.

If you come to a familiar fork in the road, remember not to repeat the painful one.

Before you do something familiar, remember to breathe.

Why play when it will spark a blaze that is hard to put out.

A lonely day is not when you're alone but when you're in a crowd and don't care.

Encourage yourself by remembering yourself.

Be an antidote when a cure is not visible.

If it hurts now imagine how bad it was when you were hiding.

If you think recovery is hard try relapse it's harder.

Not all who gamble are addicts, but all addicts are gamblers.

Addiction is not a weakness, it's a disease of the mind and body.

A consequence of recovery is living with a real world view.

Even the right path has a few bumps in it.

There are battles that are small moral victories to provide a better chance to win the war.

When fighting for right, choose your gear carefully and consider the future.

Recovery is:

>Releasing the past
>Embracing this moment.
>Continuing to grow.
>Ongoing change.

Vigilant awareness of triggers. Entering into community.
Reintegrating into life Your Hope for today.

Today is the most important day of your life!

Recovery is like finding a hidden treasure, it's more valuable than anything in the world.

When you find what you're looking for it's never too late.

To lose everything is to gain everything that's real.

If you're still alive when you reach out for help it isn't too late.

You don't have to know someone to help them, but if you don't know yourself it's harder.

When this moment is in doubt, remember you're not alone.

A mind is not wasted unless it is not used.

Addiction, disease and infection all have two things in common. They can all be treated and they can all kill.

Remembering is fluid when you are deciding on an action. But repeat mistakes tend to hurt like a solid memory.

Focus is key when trying to avoid repeating the past.

Being tempted is human, fighting temptation is divine help. The only path to recovery is through the valley of bottoming out.

Every person finds their own last time that leads to recovery.

Memorial Day can be the day of new beginnings.

Recovery is work, but when the load is shared it gets easier.

If you learn something that helps share it in your own personal way.

Bad events are part of recovery. To face them remember that many are because of the addiction.

In life it is yourself that you need in order to need others.

It is where you focus in your heart that determines the path ahead of you.

Recovery is knowing you need to change and then taking advice seriously.

The cost of someone helping you is not in money but in the heart.

To receive help you must first be honest with those who don't need help from you.

Some things stick in the memory but they don't have to control your heart.

Recovery is like cleaning your home, it needs constant attention.

I have Asthma just like I have a gambling addiction. The biggest difference is one can go into remission and the other can't.

Hating the addiction while loving the addict is especially hard when it's you.

You should never argue with yourself because you never win and the jacket they put you in is a pain to get off.

When things go south it doesn't have they don't have to crash.

Pain is temporary, life is ever changing and both are best experienced in the moment they are happening.

Memory is fleeting hold the good memories as long as possible.

Recovery is difficult but Addiction is deadly.

Change is only good if acceptance is included.

Excuses are the old addict peeking out.

When beginning recovery exhaustion is understandable. So many past lies need to be released for the truth.

When recovery begins there is growing pain.

To take the message to others who still suffer means to work on knowing your story. Remember that to tell your story is the best way for others to know theirs!

I am an official RCG. A RCG is Recovering Compulsive Gambler.

If it sounds like a person is making fun of an addiction, listen closer. They could be trying to understand themselves!

RECOVERY:

> Recurring thoughts
> Eventual understanding
> Continued focus
> Obsessive fear
> Very Scary
> Eventual awareness
> Recurrent pain
> Yearning freedom

ADDICTION:

Away from others
Don't know time
Disturbing losses
Incomprehensible losses
Continual losses
Terrible lingering
Insatiable urges
Ordered insanity
No way out

It's wise not to tell people how smart you are. It saves you embarrassment when you do something to disprove it.

Better to be so stupid that you look smart than so smart you're an idiot.

Better to solve a problem quietly than to be stumped publicly.

Can you repeat something said and make it sound like a new idea?

Waking up alive is better than sleep with fish.

A wise man once told me to keep moving. I guess Playing in the street is bad.

You can live today or die yesterday.

Tired is the condition of an addict. Exhausted is the condition of recovery.

It is better to laugh today than cry over yesterday.

When speaking, writing or responding it is often best to think of what the perspective is of the other person involved.

When choosing your words don't forget who you are talking to.

Never and always are words that often result in the opposite result as the intent.

A single kind word can carry your day just as anger can destroy it.

I AM because you are.

Living is not passive but active.

I am alive but am I living?

If you don't then who will?

Recovery is like flushing a toilet. You need to keep flushing the crap until it's gone.

Recovery involves mourning the loss of the addiction.

Addiction is like a hemorrhoid and Recovery is the cure.

Just one more time is not realistic in recovery. It means I'm ready to relapse.

Addiction is as real as recovery.

The inner addict will fight recovery so the real you needs to look for defensive tools.

Harm Reduction as a theory for addiction is comparable to putting two bullets in a revolver. It still can kill.

To watch people leaving a business, is to learn about its true colors.

There is a reason for 12 steps in programs of recovery. It can remind you that it takes time.

The Recovery program is a guide to be balanced with the Unity program, other writings and principals of life.

There is little value in ruminating on the past while avoiding today.

If all you eat is your past failures you will have little hope of tasting success.

You can go to a meeting but if you don't apply anything it will accomplish very little.

Time is most important when you're short on it.

The Path to recovery leads to a valley of peace. To get there you need to get through a mountain pass filled with dangers.

Don't be flushed down the sewer by your past. Let today lift you up.

A step can either be forward or backward. Which way will you go?

When Making changes falling down happens. Getting back up is important.

Recovery is forever. Addiction does not have to be.

Be honest with yourself and you have more hope for recovery.

A yapping dog can help an addict more than a person playing 'recovery games'.

Be who you are in recovery it will change everything in time.

Recovery is knowing relapse as well as the disease.

A rabbit hole only fits if you go down it.

Don't be a monkey see person, it won't be a barrel of fun.

Winning comes at a great expense. Is it worth it to you?

If you think you have a system, consider the results.

Put one foot forward and you will see what is happening around you.

It isn't what we want that is most important but what we need.

Time is not the factor that determines wisdom it is experiences.

Sometimes the wrong answer is the solution to a problem.

One step can make all the difference.

Your perspective is determined by your seating position.

Frustration is temporary. How we respond can cause permanent impressions.

One step at a time is not always the same.

A vision of wins is a recipe for disaster.

Money does not a compulsive gambler make. It is all about the action.

Waking up from a scary dream is good unless it is all a dream.

There is no time like today to let go of the past so you can embrace tomorrow.

Holding onto yesterday keeps you from seeing today.

The path to change is yours to walk.

It only takes a split second to change a lifetime.

The pain of the past can help you better in the present only if you let it be in the Past.

Painful memories are not present events.

Recovery is a challenge to change.

Addiction eats reality but recovery builds a future.

If you recognize your mistakes you are becoming wiser each time.

In life family is both biological and spiritual.

Life is fluid and changing.

Addiction, anxiety, depression and low self-esteem are often connected.

Recovery is like a convertible, when the urge to relapse calls you need to put up the roof.

Addiction is like thirst.

Recovery begins when self-pity is let go for a determination to commit to the work necessary.

Patience and impatience are not all that different to addicts in recovery.

Recovery is about talking with others and self-education.

Be aware of conversational and environmental triggers when in recovery.

The longest journey is one that goes nowhere.

The path to the heart should not be taken lightly.

To run is best when it's away from trouble.

Alone in recovery is not good because recovery is relationship.

Addiction is Alone and recovery is relationship.

I used to cry because of my addiction, now I cry because others are missing out on recovery

A broken heart in recovery is because of those not at the meeting yet.

Making change personal makes it more likely to be successful.

Making change personal makes it more likely to be successful.

Family is important, defining it can be difficult though.

Just as a person can get over confident in recovery, so it is with meetings.

Consider the difference between what is real and what is imagined.

Time outs are for pets, children and addicts in recovery.

Sometimes caring can be scary.

Recovery may have bumps in the road, but addiction is a deep hole that takes a lot of help to escape.

If you don't get into the cocoon of early recovery, you'll miss the process of becoming a butterfly in later recovery.

In life we sometimes need to get an attitude trim.

A slip happens but it takes effort to fall.

To protect yourself you must first know what the problem is.

To know the truth you need to recognize a lie first.

Breathing in recovery is accepting today.

In recovery as in business it is not wise to say something without being sure of it.

Recovery requires an intense desire to focus on this moment clean!

A colon can indicate a pause, painful stoppage or the runs. It's all in your perspective.

If you have to go, let it be to the bathroom.

Recovery is letting go not bringing it up.

When you run out of strength it is important to remember you are not alone.

Today is lived one breath at a time. Yesterday has already been exhaled. Don't try to revive it.

Everything you did to gamble just shows what you can do for recovery.

At this moment you are not alone even if no one is with you.

Inhale and exhale then move on.

To get through a day clean find your own thought. It only needs to make sense to you.

Every moment of life is what you make of it. Don't under value it.

The road is not wide and easy that leads to the best things in life.

Addiction is an attic and recovery is a family room.

If you gamble a little you may never stop.

To change your path requires different moccasins.

Recovery involves more than addicts.

If you climb a rotting tree it will fail you sooner or later.

Running backwards makes seeing where you're going almost impossible.

Your story is as important as any other, don't be afraid to share it honestly.

If you lie to yourself you won't know it unless you hear the truth.

Remember your past but live your present.

Be careful who you follow they might be lost.

It took time to do the damage so it will take time to recover.

Addiction is like a weak bladder. It just keeps going.

A winning gambler is like weight loss at an all you can eat buffet.

Recovery is like hand washing dishes. You need to keep at it or everything piles up.

Recovery requires continued expulsion of the mucus of addiction.

Our life savings include more than money. The people, experiences and today are priceless and aren't lost.

At your lowest point you are not as alone as you think.

Remember that you're not perfect and recovery is a process.

You can't clean dishes in a toilet and recovery is not about past crap either.

Review, Evaluate, Consider, Organize, Value, Explore, Restore, You. That is RECOVERY.

The length of a struggle is determined by the secrets you keep from yourself.

Early in recovery the anxiety on the unknown is strong.

In recovery wealth should not be measured by the money you have, but by the live you are living.

On line gambling is selling your house by paying the buyer for it.

Recovery is finding the real world after being in the 'matrix'.

I lost my addiction to recovery. Now I have more friends.

On order to make changes you must first know the target.

Life is measured in the mistakes conquered.

If you go to bed in one room and wake up in another, you might have a problem.

Addicts are best in action. When in recovery the action is clean time sensitive.

No desire to gamble is sometimes code for I have a plan.

If you truly want to change, you will focus on your pockets first.

In recovery you should get rid of your inner chameleon.

An honest answer is tied to a tricky question.

I am here, you are here But where is HERE?

If you focus on fear you may miss the joy.

SCARED is Supporting Continued Addiction Refined Every Day.

HOPE is Having Open Plans Explained.

Words are only as good as the actions behind them.

A picture may be worth a thousand words, but actions are priceless!

One moment clean is better than a thousand addicted.

Being exhausted is a sign of recovery.

Be determined rather than let yourself be determined by the past.

Any challenge is only as hard as the number of people going through it with you.

Yesterday isn't today.

Know your underlying health and you will know your path.

What you do now determines if you are sober now.

Bernard Zeitler

THE AUTHOR

Bernard Zeitler is a compulsive gambler. He has been in recovery since November 21, 2007. His chosen form of gambling was lottery tickets, which are sold at many retailers. Until March 15, 2011, he sold lottery tickets as a part of his job at a convenience store. At the end of October 2007, he was on the verge of losing his job and spent time in an adult Psych. unit for suicidal depression as a result of his addiction. He has a Bachelor's Degree in Social Work with a minor in Psychology which was received in 1991 and has worked in various areas of the mental health field. He spends time studying fundamentals of recovery. It is his hope and dream to create a program for compulsive gamblers that works with the whole family and has some form of housing for the compulsive gambler while starting their recovery.

He is the Author of:

"How To Win As A High Roller While Losing Your Shirt"

"The 30 Detox For Gamblers"

"After Detox: The Next 90 Days"

"The Life Recovery Journal"

"The Path To Recovery Program"

"Why Me?"

"The Humorous Life"

This book is a compilation of his 4 standalone books for Recovery. He continues to work on different projects in the area of Compulsive Gambling and hopes to continue bringing hope and recovery to those who are suffering with this Problem.

Made in the USA
Lexington, KY
27 January 2018